Nick Vandome

# Mac Computing
# for Seniors

2nd Edition

In easy steps is an imprint of In Easy Steps Limited
4 Chapel Court · 42 Holly Walk · Leamington Spa
Warwickshire · United Kingdom · CV32 4YS
www.ineasysteps.com

Second Edition

In Easy Steps Limited supports The Forest Stewardship Council (FSC),
the leading international forest certification organisation. All our titles
that are printed on Greenpeace approved FSC certified paper carry the
FSC logo.

**Mixed Sources**
Product group from well-managed
forests and other controlled sources
www.fsc.org  Cert no. SGS-COC-005998
© 1996 Forest Stewardship Council

Printed and bound in the United Kingdom

ISBN 978-1-84078-434-3

# Contents

## 9 Mac Mobility 151

## 10 Expanding Your Horizons 159

## 11 Safety Net 177

## Index 187

# 1 Introduction

Mac computers are renowned for their ease-of-use, stability and security, with good reason. They are an excellent option for anyone, particularly senior users, since they usually do exactly what is required of them. This chapter introduces the range of Macs and shows how you can add your own personalization.

# Life and Times of Apple

Apple, the makers of Mac computers, was founded in California in 1976 by Steve Jobs, Steve Wozniak and Ronald Wayne. Originally called Apple Computer the initial emphasis of the company was very much on personal computers. After some innovative early machines, Steve Jobs decided that the next Apple computer had to have a Graphical User Interface (GUI). This is a computer that can be controlled by the user with a device such as a mouse or a joystick. In many ways this was the breakthrough that has shaped the modern face of personal computing.

The first Macintosh computer, using a GUI, was released in 1984. The sales of the first Mac were good, particularly because of its strength using graphics and for desktop publishing. However, shortly afterwards Steve Jobs left Apple which was the beginning of a downturn for the company. Although the introduction of the first PowerBook was a success, the increasing development of Microsoft Windows and IBM-compatible PCs became a real threat to the existence of Apple.

## The rise of the iMac

During the 1990s, Apple experienced several commercial setbacks and the company was in trouble. However, shortly afterwards Steve Jobs returned to Apple and in 1998, the iMac was launched. Apple had always been known for its stylish design but the iMac took this to a new level. With its all-in-one design and bright, translucent colors it transformed people's attitudes towards personal computers.

The iMac got Apple back on its commercial feet and this was followed in 2001 by the iPod, a portable digital music player. Like the iMac this caught the public's imagination and Apple have exploited this with dramatic effect with the addition of products such as iTunes, iPhone, iPad and their OS X operating system. The death of Steve Jobs in October 2011 created a potential challenge for Apple but his legacy, in terms of the range of innovative products that he introduced, has left it strongly positioned in the market.

**Don't forget**

Mac users are usually very devoted to the Apple brand and support it with very enthusiastic fervor.

8

# Choosing a Mac

As with most things in the world of technology there is a wide range of choice when it comes to buying a Mac computer. This includes the top of the range Mac Pro, which is a very powerful desktop computer, to the MacBook Air, which is a laptop that is thin enough to fit into an envelope (if required!). In between these two extremes are a variety of desktops and laptops that can match most people's computing needs. For the senior user some of the best options are:

## Desktop

As a good, all-purpose, desktop computer the iMac is hard to beat. This is the machine that helped to turn around Apple's fortunes in the 1990s and it remains one of their most popular computers.

The iMac is a self-contained computer which means the hard drive and the monitor are housed together as a single unit. There are a variety of models that offer different levels of computing power and different monitor sizes. At the time of writing, all models have a DVD writer and come with wireless connectivity for connection to the Internet.

Another desktop option is the Mac Mini, which is a smaller, cheaper, computer that consists of just the hard drive. This means that you have to buy the mouse, keyboard and monitor separately. This is a reasonable option if your computing needs are mainly email, the Internet and word processing. For anything more, the iMac is a better option.

## Laptop

More and more people are using laptops these days, as mobile computing takes over from static desktops. In the Mac range, the MacBook is probably the best all-round option. Although not as powerful as the iMac, it has enough computing power for most people's needs. The MacBook Pro is aimed at the business market and the MacBook Air, designed with revolutionary thinness, is aimed at the consumer market for those on the move.

**Don't forget**

All new Macs come with the latest Mac operating system pre-installed. At the time of writing this is OS X (pronounced 10), or 10.7 to be precise, known as Lion (see next page for details).

**Don't forget**

If you plan on traveling a lot with a laptop, the MacBook Air may feel a bit too slight due to its very thin design. However, it is surprisingly robust.

# The Mac Operating System

The Mac operating system (the software that is the foundation of how the computer works) is known as OS X (pronounced 10). This is now on version 10.7, which is more commonly known as Lion.

Apple is renowned for designing operating systems that are easy to use, robust and more secure than their Windows-based PC counterparts. The OS X operating system is based on UNIX, a system that is both secure and has stood the test of time.

OS X is not only easy to use it also has a very attractive graphical interface. This is created by a technology known as Quartz and the interface itself is known as Aqua, which is a set of graphics based on the theme of water.

The OS X Lion interface is immediately eye-catching as soon as any Mac is turned on:

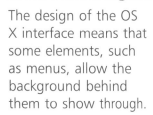

**Don't forget**

The design of the OS X interface means that some elements, such as menus, allow the background behind them to show through.

**Hot tip**

To find out more about your current operating system, click on the Apple symbol at the top left of the screen and click on About This Mac.

# Ports and Slots Explained

Every Mac computer has a number of ports and slots for different functions to be performed or additional devices to be attached.

### DVD/CD slot
This is the slot into which DVDs or CDs can be inserted to play their content. It can also be used to burn content onto blank DVDs or CDs. This slot is at the side or front of the computer, depending on the type and model of the Mac.

**Don't forget**

USB stands for Universal Serial Bus.

### USB ports
These are the ports that are used to connect a variety of external devices such as digital cameras, memory card readers, pen drives or external hard drives. On most Macs there are a minimum of two USB ports.

### Firewire ports
These are similar to USB ports but they are generally used for devices that are required to transfer larger amounts of data. One of the most common uses for Firewire is the transfer of digital video. Firewire ports look similar to USB ones except they are slightly chunkier.

### Thunderbolt
This is a port for transferring data at high speeds, up to 12 times faster than Firewire. It can also be used to connect a Thunderbolt screen to a MacBook

### Ethernet
This is for the connection of an Ethernet cable for a cable or broadband Internet connection.

# The Mac Desktop

The first thing to do with your new Mac is to turn it on. This is done by pressing this button once.

The first thing you will see is the Mac desktop. This is the default layout and, as we will see in the next few pages, this can be customized to your own preferences.

Some of the specific elements of the desktop are:

Apple Menu            Finder Menu bars

Dock                  The Finder          Background

**Don't forget**

If the Finder is not showing, click on this icon on the Dock. The Dock is the collection of icons at the bottom of the screen.

# Customizing Your Mac

All of us have different ideas about the way we want our computers set up, in terms of layout, colors, size and graphics. Macs allow a great deal of customization so that you can personalize it to genuinely make it feel like your own computer.

The customization features are contained within the System Preferences. To access these:

1 Click here on the Dock (the full workings of the Dock will be covered in detail in Chapter Two)

2 The System Preferences folder contains a variety of functions that can be used to customize your Mac (see following pages for details)

Hot tip

Click on the Show All button at the top of the System Preferences folder to show all of the items in the folder, regardless of which element you are currently using.

# Changing the Background

Background imagery is an important way to add your own personal touch to your Mac. (This is the graphical element upon which all other items on your computer sit.) There are a range of background options that can be used. To select your own background:

1   Click on this icon in the System Preferences folder

14

2   Click on the Desktop tab

3   Select a location from where you want to select a background

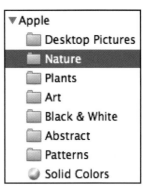

4   Click on one of the available backgrounds

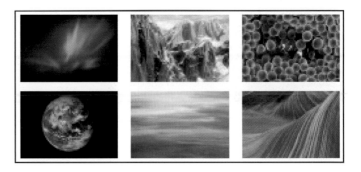

5   The background is applied as the desktop background imagery

# Changing the Screen Saver

A screen saver is the element that appears when the Mac has not been used for a specified period of time. Originally this was designed to avoid screen burn (caused by items being at the same position on the screen for an extended period of time) but now they are largely a graphical element. To select your own screen saver:

**1** Click on this icon in the System Preferences folder

**2** Click on the Screen Saver tab **Screen Saver**

**3** Select a location from where you want to select a screen saver

**4** Click the Test button to preview the selected screen saver

**Test**

**5** Drag this slider to specify the amount of time the Mac is inactive before the screen saver is activated

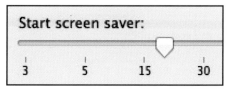

15

**Don't forget**

Screen savers were originally designed to prevent screen burn (areas of the screen becoming marked as a result of elements remaining static for a prolonged period of time), but now they are more for cosmetic graphical purposes.

# Changing the Screen Size

For most computer users the size at which items are displayed on the screen is a crucial issue: if items are too small this can make them hard to read and lead to eye strain; too large and you have to spend a lot of time scrolling around to see everything.

The size of items on the screen is controlled by the screen's resolution i.e. the number of colored dots displayed in an area of the screen. The higher the resolution the smaller the items on the screen, the lower the resolution the larger the items. To change the screen resolution:

**Don't forget**

A higher resolution makes items appear sharper on the screen, even though they appear physically smaller.

**16**

**1** Click on this icon in the System Preferences folder

Displays

**2** Select a resolution setting to change the overall screen resolution

**Resolutions:**

1280 × 800
1152 × 720
1024 × 768
1024 × 768 (stretched)
1024 × 640

**3** Click here to select the number of colors displayed on the screen (the higher the better)

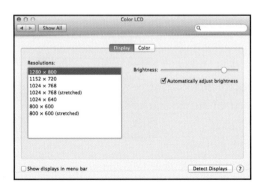

# Changing the Text Size

Another way to change the size of items on the screen is through the Universal Access options within the System Preferences folder. This is a range of options for users who have difficulties with seeing, hearing or mobility when using the mouse and keyboard. To use the Universal Access options for changing the size of text:

**1** Click on this icon in the System Preferences folder

**2** Click on the Seeing tab

**3** Click on the On button to activate the zoom function

Zoom:

(●) On ( ) Off

**4** Press these keys to zoom in on any items on the screen. Use the mouse to move around the zoomed items

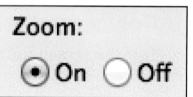

**5** Click here if you prefer white text on a black background

Display:

( ) Black on white
(●) White on black

Beware
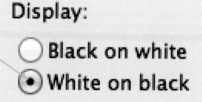

White text on a black background can become irritating after a period of time, unless you need to use it for a specific reason.

# Adjusting the Volume

For users with hearing difficulties there are options for setting the screen to flash if there is an alert sound on the system. To do this:

**1** Click on this icon in the System Preferences folder

Universal Access

**2** Click on the Hearing tab

Hearing

**3** Check on this box to activate the screen to flash whenever there is an alert sound

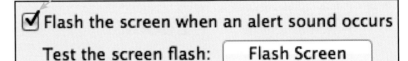

☑ **Flash the screen when an alert sound occurs**

**Test the screen flash:** Flash Screen

**4** Click on this button to test the Flash Screen effect

**5** Click on this button to access the Sound folder

Adjust Volume...

**6** Drag this slider to change the overall volume

Output volume: ◀ ⬤ ◀))  ☐ Mute

**Don't forget**

The volume on a Mac can also be adjusted by clicking on the loudspeaker icon that appears at the top of the screen on the Finder toolbar. For more information about the Finder see Chapter Two.

18

# Customizing the Mouse

If you have any kinds of mobility problems in your hands it can be difficult to use a mouse. To use options to make this easier:

**1** Click on this icon in the System Preferences folder

**2** Drag this slider to change the Tracking Speed (this is the speed at which the cursor moves across the screen)

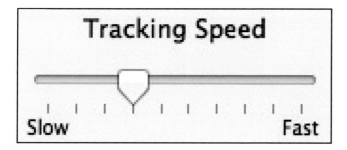

The Tracking Speed for a trackpad can be set within the Trackpad System Preference. Click on the Point & Click tab to access the Tracking Speed option.

**3** Drag this slider to change the Double-Click Speed (this is the speed at which you have to consecutively click the mouse button to activate any double-click actions)

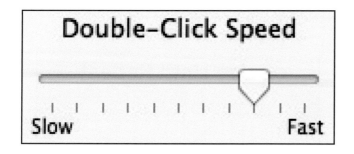

# Customizing the Keyboard

As with the mouse, or trackpad, it is possible to customize a Mac keyboard so that it is easier to use for anyone with mobility problems in their hands. To do this:

**1** Click on this icon in the System Preferences folder

**2** Click on the Keyboard tab

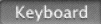

**3** Drag this slider to change the Key Repeat Rate (this is the speed a key stroke will repeat if the key is held down)

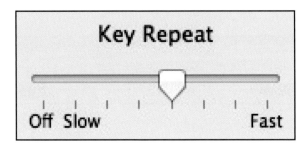

**Hot tip**

Click on the Keyboard Shortcuts tab in the Keyboard window to access options for keyboard shortcuts for certain functions. The assigned keys can be changed if required.

**4** Drag this slider to change the Delay Until Repeat option (this is the time it will take for a key stroke to be repeated if a key is held down. If it is set to Off, a key stroke will not be repeated until the key is released and then pressed again)

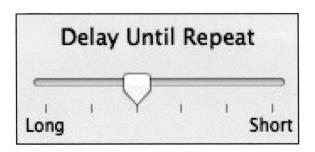

# Sharing with Windows

### General sharing

One of the historical complaints about Macs is that it is difficult to share files between them and Microsoft Windows computers. While this may have been true with some file types in years gone by, this is an issue that is becoming less and less important. Some of the reasons for this are:

- A number of popular file formats, such as PDFs (Portable Document Format) for documents and JPEGs (Joint Photographic Experts Group) for photos and images, are designed so that they can be used on both Mac and Windows platforms

- A lot of software programs on the Mac have options for saving files into different formats, including ones that are specifically for Windows machines

- Other popular programs, such as Microsoft Office, now have Mac versions and the resulting files can be shared on both formats

### Sharing with Boot Camp

For people who find it hard to live without Microsoft Windows, help is at hand even on a Mac. Macs have a program called Boot Camp that can be used to run a version of Windows on a Mac. This is available with the latest version of the Mac OS X operating system, Lion. Once it has been accessed, a copy of Windows can then be installed and run. This means that if you have a non-Mac program that you want to use on your Mac, you can do so with Boot Camp.

Boot Camp is set up with the Boot Camp Assistant which is located within the Utilities folder within the Applications folder. Once this is run you can then install either Windows XP, Vista or 7, which will run at its native speed.

**Don't forget**

Other than for some games, the issue of sharing files between Macs and Windows PCs, and vice versa, have largely disappeared.

# Shutting Down and Sleeping

When you are not using your Mac you will want to either shut it down or put it to sleep. If you shut it down this will close all of your applications and open files. This is the best option if you are not going to be returning to your Mac for a reasonable length of time (say, more than one day).

If you put the Mac to sleep, it will retain your current work session so that you can continue when you wake up the Mac. This option is useful if you know you will be returning to your Mac within a few hours.

The process for shutting down or sleeping a Mac is very similar in both cases:

 Click on this icon on the main Menu bar

Click on either Sleep or Shut Down...

## Hot tip

Check on the 'Reopen windows when logging back in' box when you shut down. This ensures that the next time you turn on your Mac, it will resume at the place where you closed it i.e. all open programs and files will appear in their previous state.

If you are shutting down, a window appears asking you to confirm your request

Click on the Shut Down button

# 2 Finding Your Way Around

This chapter looks at two of the vital elements on the Mac, the Finder and the Dock. It shows how to use these to access and view items. It also shows how to work with different windows and organize your desktop. It also covers some new ways to navigate with your computer and introduces the Mac App Store.

# Finder: the Core of Your Mac

One of the most basic requirements of any computer is that you can easily and quickly find the applications and documents which you want to use. On Macs, a lot of this work is done through the aptly named Finder. This is the area on your Mac which you can use to store, organize and display files, folders and applications. It is an area that you will return to frequently whenever you are using your Mac. To access the Finder:

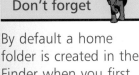
**1** Click on this icon on the Dock (this is one element of the Dock that cannot be removed)

**2** The Finder window has a Sidebar and a main window area

**3** The Sidebar can be used to create folders and categories for a variety of items

**4** The main window displays items within the selected location

## Using the Sidebar

The Sidebar is the left-hand panel of the Finder which can be used to access items on your Mac:

**1** Click on a button on the Sidebar

**2** Its contents are displayed in the main Finder window

**Don't forget**

When you click on an item in the Sidebar, its contents are shown in the main Finder window to the right.

## Adding to the Sidebar

Items that you access most frequently can be added to the Sidebar. To do this:

**1** Drag an item from the main Finder window onto the Sidebar

**2** The item is added to the Sidebar. You can do this with programs, folders and files

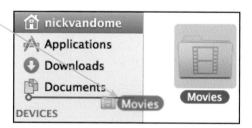

**Don't forget**

Items can be removed from the Sidebar by dragging them away from it. They then disappear in a satisfying puff of smoke. This does not remove the item from your Mac, just the Finder Sidebar.

...cont'd

## Viewing items in the Finder

Items within the Finder can be viewed in a number of different ways:

**1** Click on this button to view items as icons

**Hot tip**

In Icons view it is possible to view the icons at different sizes. To do this, click on the wheel icon next to the view icon and select Show View Options. Then drag the Icon size slider for the appropriate size.

**2** Click on this button to view items as a list

| Name ▲ |
|---|
| ▶ 🗂 Desktop |
| ▶ 🗋 Documents |
| ▶ 🔽 Downloads |
| ▶ 🎞 Movies |
| ▶ 🎵 Music |
| ▶ 🖼 Pictures |
| ▶ 🔶 Public |
| ▶ 🌐 Sites |

**3** Click on this button to view items in columns

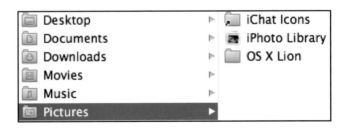

# Quick Look

Through a Finder option called Quick Look, it is possible to view the content of a file without having to first open it. To do this:

**1** Select a file within the Finder

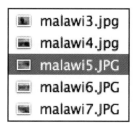

malawi3.jpg
malawi4.jpg
malawi5.JPG
malawi6.JPG
malawi7.JPG

**2** Press the space bar

**3** The contents of the file are displayed without it opening in its default program

27

malawi5.JPG    Open with Preview

**4** Click on the cross to close Quick Look

# Covers

Covers is an innovative feature on the Mac that enables you to view the contents of a folder without having to open the folder. Additionally, each item is displayed as a large icon that enables you to see what a particular item contains, such as images. To use Covers:

1     Select a folder and at the top of the Finder window click on this button

2     The items within the folder are displayed in their cover state

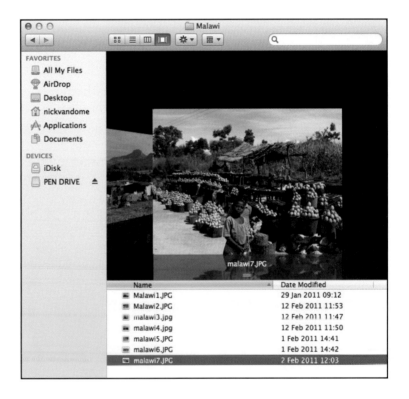

3     Drag with the mouse on each item to view the next one, or click on the slider at the bottom of the window

# Using the Dock

The Dock is the collection of icons that, by default, appears along the bottom of the desktop. If you choose, this can stay visible permanently. The Dock is a way to quickly access the programs and folders that you use most frequently. The two main things to remember about the Dock are:

- It is divided into two: programs go on the left of the dividing line; all other items go on the right

- It can be edited in just about any way you choose

Hot tip

Items on the Dock can be activated by clicking on them once, rather than double-clicking.

By default the Dock appears at the bottom of the screen.

...cont'd

## Customizing the Dock

The Dock can be modified in numerous ways. This can affect both the appearance of the Dock and the way it operates. To set Dock preferences:

**Don't forget**

The Apple Menu is accessed from the apple icon that is always visible at the top left of the screen.

**1** Select Apple Menu>Dock from the Menu bar

**2** Select one of the options for how the Dock is displayed on the screen

| Turn Hiding On | ⌥⌘D |
| Turn Magnification On | |
| | |
| Position on Left | |
| ✓ Position on Bottom | |
| Position on Right | |
| | |
| Dock Preferences... | |

**Beware**

If you select the Turn Hiding On option for the Dock then it is hidden unless you pass the cursor over the bottom of the screen (or wherever it is hidden). However, this can become annoying as the Dock then appears and disappears at times you do not want it to.

**3** Click on Dock Preferences... to access more options for customizing the Dock

**Dock Preferences...**

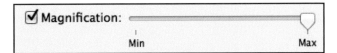

**4** Check on the Magnification box and drag this slider to specify how much larger an icon becomes when the cursor is passed over it

## Adding and removing items

To add items to the Dock:

**1** For programs, drag their icon onto the Dock to the left of the dividing line

**2** For folders or files, drag their icon onto the Dock to the right of the dividing line

**31**

**3** To remove items from the Dock, drag them off the Dock and they disappear in a satisfying puff of smoke

## Dock menus

Each Dock item has its own contextual menu that has commands relevant to that item. To access these:

**1** Click and hold beneath a Dock item

| Options ▶ | ✓ Keep in Dock |
| Show All Windows | Open at Login |
| Hide | Show in Finder |
| Quit | |

**2** The contextual menu is displayed next to the Dock item. Click on a command as required

...cont'd

## Stacking items

To save space on the Dock it is possible to add folders to the Dock, from where their contents can be accessed. This is known as Stacks. By default, Stacks for documents and downloaded files are created on the Dock. To use Stacks:

**1** Stacked items are placed at the right-hand side of the Dock

**2** Click on a Stack to view its contents

**3** Stacks can be viewed as a grid, or

4  As a fan, depending on the
   number of items it contains

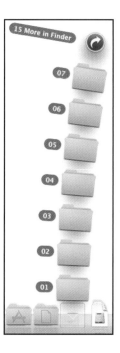

5  Click on an item within a Stack to open it

6  To create a new Stack, drag a folder onto the Dock.
   Any new items that are added to the folder will also
   be visible through the Stack

# Mission Control

Mission Control is a function in OS X Lion that helps you organize all of your open apps, full-screen apps and documents. It also enables you to quickly view the Dashboard and Desktop. Within Mission Control there are also Spaces, where you can group together similar types of documents. To use Mission Control:

**1** Click on this button on the Dock

**2** All open files and apps are visible via Mission Control

**34**

**3** Desktop items are grouped together on the top row within Mission Control within an area called a Space. Position the cursor over the right-hand corner and click on the plus sign to add a new Space. Drag items from the desktop onto the new Space

**4** If there is more than one window open for an app they will be grouped together by Mission Control

Safari

**Beware**

Any apps or files that have been minimized or closed do not appear within the main Mission Control window. Instead they are located to the right of the dividing line on the Dock.

35

**5** If an app is made full-screen (see pages 42–43) it automatically appears along the top row

Safari          Preview

# Working with Mac Windows

When you are working with a lot of open windows it can sometimes be confusing about which is the active window and how you can then quickly switch to other windows.

**1** The active window always sits on the top of any other open windows. There can only be one active window at any one time

**2** Click on any window behind the currently active one, to bring it to the front and make it active

**3** At the top left of any active window, click on the red button to close it, the amber button to minimize it and the green button to enlarge it

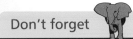

# Launchpad

Even though the Dock can be used to store shortcuts to your applications, it is limited in terms of space. The full set of applications on your Mac can be found in the Finder but OS X Lion introduced a new feature that allows you to quickly access and manage all of your applications.
These include the ones that are pre-installed on your Mac and also any that you install yourself or download from the Apple App Store. This feature is called Launchpad. To use it:

1. Click once on this button on the Dock

**Don't forget**

To launch an app from within Launchpad, click on it once.

2. All of the apps (applications) are displayed

3. Similar types of apps can be grouped together in individual folders. By default, the Utilities are grouped in this way

# Mac Apps

In addition to the Launchpad, Mac programs (apps) are located in the Applications folder. This is located within the Finder. To view and access the available programs:

**1** Click on the Applications button in the Finder

Programs can be added to the Dock by dragging their icon there from the Applications folder.

**2** The currently installed programs are displayed

**3** To open a program, double-click on its icon

# The App Store

The App Store is another OS X app. This is an online facility where you can download and buy new apps. These cover a range of categories such as productivity, business and entertainment. When you select or buy an app from the App Store, it is downloaded automatically by Launchpad and appears here next to the rest of the apps.

To buy apps from the App Store you need to have an Apple ID and account. If you have not already set this up, it can be done when you first access the App Store. To use the App Store:

**Don't forget**

The App Store is an online function so you will need an Internet connection with which to access it.

**1** Click on this icon on the Dock or within the Launchpad

**Hot tip**

You can set up an Apple ID when you first set up your Mac or you can do it when you register for the App Store or the iTunes Store.

**2** The homepage of the App Store contains the current top featured apps

**3** Your account information and quick link categories are listed at the right-hand side of the page

# Downloading Apps

The App Store contains a wide range of apps: from small, fun apps, to powerful productivity ones. However, downloading them from the App Store is the same regardless of the type of app. The only differences are whether they require to be paid for or not and the length of time they take to download. To download an app from the App Store:

1 Browse through the App Store until you find the required app

2 Click on the app to view a detailed description about it

**40**

3 Click on the button underneath the app icon to download it. If there is no charge for the app the button will say Free

4 If there is a charge for the app, the button will say Buy App

5 Click on the Install App button

6 Enter your Apple ID account details to continue downloading the app

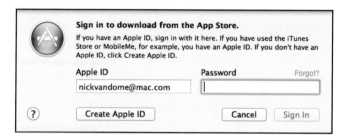

**Sign in to download from the App Store.**
If you have an Apple ID, sign in with it here. If you have used the iTunes Store or MobileMe, for example, you have an Apple ID. If you don't have an Apple ID, click Create Apple ID.

Apple ID
nickvandome@mac.com

Password          Forgot?

Create Apple ID          Cancel    Sign In

7 The progress of the download is displayed in a progress bar underneath the Launchpad icon on the Dock

8 Once it has been downloaded, the app is available within Launchpad

TextEdit          Time Machine

Pages          SoundCloud

**Don't forget**

Depending on their size, different apps take differing amounts of time to be downloaded.

**Don't forget**

As you download more apps, additional pages will be created within the Launchpad to accommodate them.

41

# Full-Screen Apps

When working with apps we all like to be able to see as much of a window as possible. With OS X Lion this is now possible with the full-screen app. This allows you to expand an app with this functionality so that it takes up the whole of your monitor or screen with a minimum of toolbars visible. Some apps have this functionality but some do not. To use full-screen apps:

**1** By default an app appears on the desktop with other windows behind it

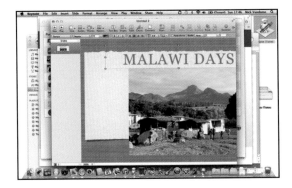

**Don't forget**

If the button in Step 2 is not visible then the app does not have the full-screen functionality.

**2** Click on this button at the top right-hand corner of the app's window

**3** The app is expanded to take up the whole window. The main Apple Menu bar and the Dock are hidden

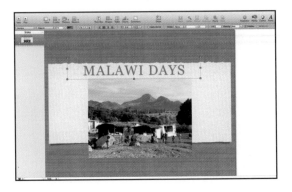

4 To view the
main Menu
bar, move the
cursor over the
top of the screen

5 You can move between all full-screen apps by
swiping with three fingers left or right on a trackpad
or Magic Mouse (see next page)

6 Move the cursor over the top right-hand
corner of the screen and click on this button
to close the full-screen functionality

7 In Mission Control all of the open full-screen apps
are shown in the top row

# A New Way of Navigating

One of the most revolutionary features of OS X Lion is the ways in which you can navigate around your applications, web pages and documents. This involves a much greater reliance on swiping on a trackpad or adapted mouse: techniques that have been imported from the iPhone and the iPad. These are known as multi-touch gestures and to take full advantage of these you will need to have one of the following devices:

- A trackpad. This will be found on new MacBooks

- A Magic Trackpad. This can be used with an iMac, a Mac Mini or a Mac Pro. It works wirelessly via Bluetooth

- A Magic Mouse. This can be used with an iMac, a Mac Mini or a Mac Pro. It works wirelessly via Bluetooth

All of these devices work using a swiping technique with fingers moving over their surface. This should be done with a light touch; it is a gentle swipe, rather than any pressure being applied to the device.

The trackpads and Magic Mouse do not have any buttons in the same way as traditional devices. Instead specific areas are clickable so that you can still perform left and right click operations.

### No more scroll bars

Another innovation in OS X Lion is the removal of scroll bars that are constantly visible on a web page or document. Instead, there are scroll bars that only appear when you are moving around a page or document. When you stop, the scroll bars melt way. Scrolling is done by multi-touch gestures on a trackpad or Magic Mouse.

By default, you can scroll through web pages or documents by swiping up or down with two fingers on a trackpad, Magic Trackpad or Magic Mouse. The full list of these multi-touch gestures is shown on page 47.

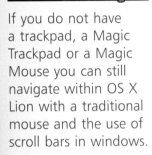

**Don't forget**

If you do not have a trackpad, a Magic Trackpad or a Magic Mouse you can still navigate within OS X Lion with a traditional mouse and the use of scroll bars in windows.

# Multi-Touch Preferences

Some multi-touch gestures only have a single action, which cannot be changed. However, others have options for changing the action for a specific gesture. This is done within the Trackpad preferences, where a full list of multi-touch gestures is shown:

## Point & Click Preferences

**1** Access the System Preferences and click on the Trackpad button

**2** Click on the Point & Click tab

**3** The actions are described on the left, with a graphic explanation on the right

**4** If there is a down arrow next to an option, click on it to change the way an action is activated

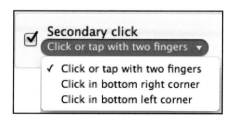

**Hot tip**

When setting multi-touch preferences try to avoid having too many gestures using the same number of fingers, in case some of them override the others.

...cont'd

## Scroll & Zoom Preferences

**1** Click on the Scroll & Zoom tab      Scroll & Zoom

**2** The actions are described on the left, with a graphic explanation on the right

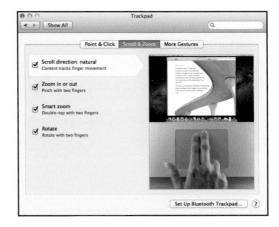

## More Gestures Preferences

**1** Click on the More Gestures tab      More Gestures

**2** The actions are described on the left, with a graphic explanation on the right

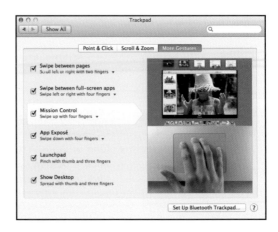

## Multi-Touch Gestures

The full list of multi-touch gestures, with their default action are:

### Point & Click

- Tap to click — tap with one finger
- Secondary click — click or tap with two fingers
- Look up — double-tap with three fingers
- Three finger drag — move with three fingers

### Scroll & Zoom

- Scroll direction: natural — content tracks finger movement. Swipe with two fingers up or down
- Zoom in or out — pinch or spread with two fingers
- Smart zoom — double-tap with two fingers
- Rotate — rotate with two fingers

### More Gestures

- Swipe between pages — scroll left or right with two fingers
- Swipe between full-screen apps — swipe left or right with three fingers
- Access Mission Control — swipe up with three fingers
- App Exposé — swipe down with three fingers
- Access Launchpad — pinch with thumb and three fingers
- Show Desktop — spread with thumb and three fingers

# Removing Items

As you work on your Mac you will have some files, folders and programs that you definitely want to keep and others that you would like to remove. To do this:

**1** In the Finder, click on the item you want to remove

malawi7.JPG

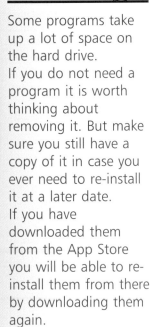
**2** Drag it onto the Trash icon on the Dock

Trash

malawi7.JPG

**3** To empty all of the items from the Trash, select Finder>Empty Trash... from the Finder Menu bar

Finder | File | Edit

About Finder

Preferences...

Empty Trash...

48

# 3 Organizing Your Mac

*Keeping everything organized on a computer can sometimes be a bit of a headache. This chapter shows you how to work confidently with files and folders on your Mac and introduces some useful items such as the Address Book and the calendar.*

# Creating Files

There are generally two ways for creating files on a Mac. One is to generate a new file within the program you are using and then save this into a folder. The other is to import files that have already been created, such as digital photographs.

### Creating new files

The process for creating new files is essentially the same for all programs:

**Don't forget**

See Chapter Four for more information on working with digital photographs.

1  Open the program you want to use

2  Select File>New from the program's Menu bar

3  Depending on the program, there may be a properties window that can be used to define various elements of the file being created

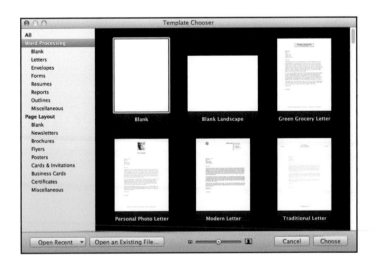

4  Add the required content to the file

# Saving Files

Once a file has been created it is essential to save it. If it is not saved then it will be lost if the Mac is turned off (although there will be a warning window that will prompt you to save any unsaved files). To save a file:

1 If a file has not been previously saved, select File>Save (or File>Save As) from the program's Menu bar

2 In the Finder, browse to the location where you want the file to be saved

**Don't forget**

It is good practice to save files as soon as they have been created, even before they have any content.

3 If the full Finder window is not showing, click on this button

**Don't forget**

Once files have been saved initially, they can then be saved using the auto-save function, (see next two pages).

4 Click on the New Folder button if you want to create a new folder for the file

**New Folder**

5 Give the file a name and click on the Save button to save the file

**Save**

# Auto Save and Versions

One of the biggest causes of frustration when working with computers is if they crash and all of your unsaved work is lost. Luckily, with OS X Lion, losing unsaved material is now a thing of the past as it includes an Auto Save function that saves work in the background as you go along. This means that you do not have to worry about having unsaved documents.

Another function within Auto Save is Versions, which enables you to revert back to previous versions of a document. To do this:

**Don't forget**

The Save a Version option is used instead of the standard Save function. Each time it is used it saves a new version of the current document or file.

**1** Create a document with content

MALAWI DAYS

**2** Select File>Save a Version from the Menu bar

| File | Edit | Insert |
| New |
| New from Theme |
| Open... |
| Open Recent |
| Close |
| Save a Version |

**3** Edit the file

4 Click on the file name and select Browse All Versions...

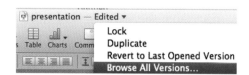

5 The current version is shown on the left-hand side and the previous versions on the right

6 Click on a previous version

7 Click on the Restore button

Restore

8 The previous version is restored as the current document

# Opening Items

It is possible to open items on your Mac from the Dock or in the Finder.

### From the Dock

**Beware**

Files can be saved onto the Desktop and opened from there. However, if there are too many items on the Desktop this can increase the time it takes the Mac to boot up and be ready for use after it has been turned on.

**1** Click on an item once to open it (program) or make it active (file)

### In the Finder

**1** Browse to the item you want to open

**2** Double-click on the required item to open it

# Creating a Folder Structure

As you create more and more files on your Mac it can become harder to find what you are looking for. To try and simplify this, it is a good idea to have a robust folder structure. This gives you a logical path to follow when you are looking for items. To create a folder structure:

1   In the Finder, click on the Documents button

2   In the main Finder window Ctrl+click and select New Folder

3   Enter a name for the new folder

Finances

4   Double-click on the new folder to open it

5   Repeat Steps 2, 3 and 4 to create as much of a folder structure as required

**Don't forget**

Macs use spring-loaded folders. This means that if you drag a file over a folder and hold it there, the folder will automatically open. As long as you keep the mouse button held down, you can do this through as many layers as there are in a folder structure.

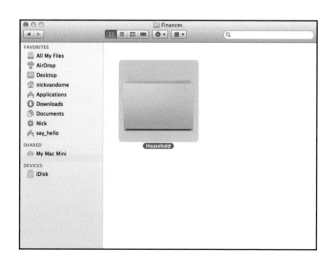

# Compiling an Address Book

Having an address book on your Mac is an excellent way to keep track of your family and friends and it can also be used within other applications, such as the Mail program for email. To create an address book:

1  Click on this icon on the Dock, or in the Launchpad

2  Click on an existing contact here

3  Their details are displayed in the right-hand window

4  Click here under the Name panel to add a new contact

5  Enter the person's details

6  Click on the Edit button to finish the entry

## Creating groups

In addition to creating individual entries in the Address Book, group contacts can also be created. This is a way of grouping contacts with similar interests. Once a group has been created, all of the entries within it can be accessed and contacted by selecting the relevant entry under the Group column. To create a group:

① Click on this button under the Group panel to create a new group entry

② Give the new group a name

> Work

③ Drag individual entries into the group (the individual entries are retained too)

> All Contacts

④ Click on a group name to view the members of the group

57

# Adding a Calendar

Electronic calendars are now a standard part of modern life and on the Mac this function is performed by the iCal program. Not only can this be used on your Mac, it can also be synchronized with other Apple devices such as an iPod or an iPhone. To create a calendar:

1. Click on this icon on the Dock, or in the Launchpad

2. Select whether to view the calendar by day, week or month

3. Click on the Today button to view the current day. Click on the forward or back arrows to move to the next day, week, month or year, depending on what is selected in Step 2

## Adding Events

To add new events:

**1** Select a date and double-click on it, or Ctrl+click on the date

**2** Select New Event

**New Event**
Paste Here

**3** Enter the details for the new event

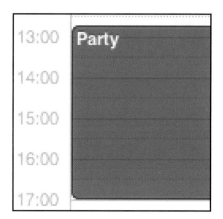

**4** Double-click on an item and select options for how it is displayed

...cont'd

### Adding a Quick Event

To add a Quick Event for a selected day:

1.  Click on this button on the top of the iCal window

2.  Enter the name of the event in the Create Quick Event box

3.  The same options as in Step 4 on the previous page are shown

### Publishing a calendar

If you have a MobileMe account you can publish calendars to it so that you can always access this information online. To do this:

1.  Select Calendar>Publish... from the iCal Menu bar

2.  Select options for how you would like to publish the calendar and click on the Publish button

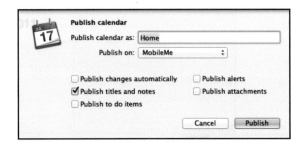

**Don't forget**

iCloud has now replaced MobileMe as the online service from Apple. However, MobileMe users can still use the service until June 2012. If you have upgraded to iCloud, the Publish option will not be available as this is done automatically by iCloud to ensure that your calendar details are always up to date.

# Using Reminders

Post-it notes are one of the great inventions of the modern world. In recognition of this the Mac has its own electronic version of this invaluable aid. To use this:

**1**     In the Finder, click on the Applications icon

**2**     Double-click on the Stickies icon

**3**     Select File>New Note from the Stickies Menu bar

**4**     Type the required note

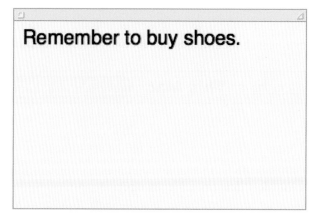

**5**     The Stickie will sit on the desktop until the program is closed

# Finding Things

Searching electronic data is now a massive industry, with companies such as Google leading the way with online searching. On Macs it is also possible to search your folders and files, using the built-in search facilities. This can be done either through the Finder or with the Spotlight program.

## Using Finder

To search for items within the Finder:

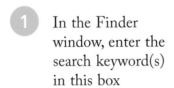

When entering search keywords try and be as specific as possible. This will cut down on the number of unwanted results.

**1** In the Finder window, enter the search keyword(s) in this box

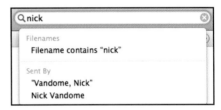

**2** The results are shown in the Finder window

**3** Select the areas over which you want the search performed

**Don't forget**

Both folders and files will be displayed in the Finder as part of the search results.

**4** Double-click on a folder to see its contents

**5** Double-click on a file to open it

**6** Click once on an item to view its file path on your computer (i.e. where it is actually located)

## Using Spotlight

Spotlight is the Mac's dedicated search program. It can be used over the files on your Mac. To use Spotlight:

**1** Click on this icon at the far right of the Finder Menu bar

**2** In the Spotlight box, enter the search keyword(s)

**3** The results are displayed according to type

**Beware**

Spotlight starts searching for items as soon as you start typing a word. So don't worry if some of the first results look inappropriate as these will disappear once you have finished typing the full word.

4  Click on an item to view it or see its contents (in the case of folders)

5  If you select a folder, it will be displayed in its location within the Finder

6  Click on the Spotlight Preferences... link

**Spotlight Preferences...**

7  Order the different content types according to how you would like them displayed in the Spotlight search results

# Adding a Printer

OS X Lion makes the printing process as simple as possible, partly by being able to automatically install new printers as soon as they are connected to your Mac. However, it is also possible to install printers manually. To do this:

**1** Open the System Preferences folder and click on the Print & Scan button

**2** Click here to add a new printer and click  on either the Add Other Printer or Scanner... link or any available printers

**3** OS X Lion loads the required printer driver (if it does not have a specific one it will try and use a generic one)

**4** The details about the printer are available in the Print & Scan window

**5** Once a printer has been installed documents can be printed by selecting File>Print from the Menu bar. Print settings can be set at this point and they can also be set by selecting File>Page/Print Setup from the Menu bar in most programs

**Beware**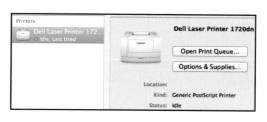

If you have an old printer your Mac may not identify it and you will have to install the print driver from the disc that came with the printer.

# External Drives

Attaching external drives is an essential part of mobile computing: whether it is to backup data as you are traveling or for downloading photos and other items. External drives are displayed on the Desktop once they have been attached and they can then be used for the required task. To do this:

**1** Attach the external drive. This is usually done with a USB cable. Once it has been attached it is shown on the Desktop

**Don't forget**

External drives can be items such as pen drives, digital cameras or external hard disks.

**2** The drive is shown under the Devices section of the Finder

**3** Perform the required task for the external drive (such as copying files or folders onto it from the hard drive of your Mac computer)

**Don't forget**

External drives can be renamed by Ctlr+clicking on their name in the Finder and overtyping it with a new name.

**4** External drives have to be ejected properly, not just pulled out or removed. To do this, click on this button next to the drive in the Finder window, or drag its icon on the Desktop over the Trash icon on the Dock. This will then change into an Eject icon

# 4 Leisure Time

Leisure time, and how we use it, is a significant issue for everyone. For Mac users this is recognized with the iLife suite of software. This chapter looks at how to use the programs within iLife to organize and edit photos, play and download music, create your own music and produce and share home movies. It also covers listening to the radio and playing chess.

# Downloading Your Photos

For users of digital cameras, iPhoto can be used to download photographs. If you do not have iPhoto, or do not want to use it, any other image editing program, such as Photoshop Elements, can be used to download digital photographs. But as iPhoto is a dedicated Mac program, this will be used for the following examples.

Photos can be downloaded by connecting your digital camera to your Mac with a USB or Firewire cable. They can also be downloaded with a card reader, into which the camera's memory card can be placed.

Once a camera has been connected to your Mac, iPhoto should open automatically. Click on the Import button to download the photos from your camera into the iPhoto Library.

**Don't forget**

iPhoto is part of the iLife suite of apps that cover items such as photos, music, web publishing and video. Access it by clicking on this icon on the Dock.

Once photographs have been downloaded by iPhoto they are displayed within the Library. This is the storage area for all of the photographs that are added to iPhoto.

From within iPhoto a variety of tasks can be performed. These include organizing, editing and sharing your photographs.

# Viewing Photos

There are a variety of ways in which photos can be viewed and displayed in iPhoto.

**1** In the main window double-click on an image

**2** This displays it at full size (click on it once to return to the main window)

**Hot tip**

Zooming right in on a photo is an excellent way to view fine detail and see if the photo is properly in focus.

**3** In the main window drag this slider to display images in the main iPhoto window at different sizes

# Slideshows

A popular way of displaying photos is through a slideshow and iPhoto can be used to produce slick and professional looking shows. To do this:

**1** Select the required images

**2** Click on the Slideshow button

**3** Select the required settings for the slideshow

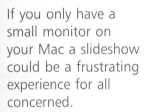
**4** Click on the Play button

**5** Move the cursor over an image and click on this button to access the Settings window

**6** The slideshow will run, with the settings specified in Step 3

# Creating a Photo Album

One of the first things to do in iPhoto is to create different albums (or folders) for your photographs. This is because the number of photographs will expand quickly and it is important to have different locations for different subject matter. This will make it a lot easier to organize your photographs and find the ones you want quickly. To create a new album:

1. Under the Source panel, click on the Add To button

2. Click on the Album button

3. Click on the New Album button

4. The untitled album appears under the Albums section

5. Enter a name for the album

...cont'd

**6** To add photos to an album, select the required ones in the main window

**7** Drag the photos into the album

**8** Click on an album to view its contents in the main iPhoto window

# Enhancing Your Photos

One of the great advantages of digital photos is that they can be edited and enhanced in numerous ways. Although iPhoto is primarily an organizational tool for digital photos, it also serves as a photo editor.

## Cropping photos

Cropping involves taking out an area of a photo behind the main subject. To do this:

**1** Select a photo

Don't forget

Most photos will benefit from some degree of cropping.

**2** Click on the Edit button and click on the Quick Fixes tab

**3** Click on the Crop button

**4** Drag on the image and drag the corner resizing handles to crop the image

**5** Click on the Done button

...cont'd

## Color adjustments

To edit the color in a photo:

**1** Select a photo

**Beware**

Be careful not to overdo color adjustments as this can give a photo an unnatural look.

**2** Click on the Edit button

**3** Click on the Adjust tab

**4** Drag the sliders to adjust the various color options in the photo

**5** The color adjustments are applied to the selected photo as they are made

**6** Click on the Adjust tab again to hide the Adjust window

## Removing red-eye

Red-eye can be a common problem when using a flash to illuminate photos of people. However, this can be removed within iPhoto:

**1** Select a photo affected by red-eye

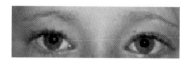

**2** Click on the Edit button

Edit

**3** Click on the Quick Fixes button

**4** Click on the Fix Red-Eye button

**5** Click on the affected area

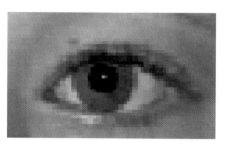

**6** The red-eye is removed

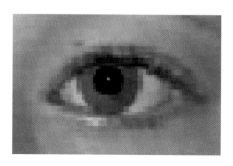

...cont'd

### Adding effects

Special effects can be added to photos in iPhoto at the touch of a button. To do this:

**1** Select a photo and click on the Edit button

**2** Click on the Effects tab

Effects

**3** Click on one of the available effects

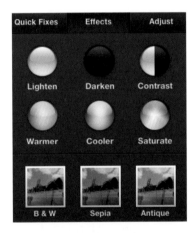

The sepia effect can create the impression of an old photo.

**4** The effect is applied to the selected photo

# Sharing and Creating

iPhoto offers a number of creative ways in which you can share your photos:

**1** Click on the Share button to access options for sharing your photos to popular sharing and social networking sites

Don't forget

The Order Prints button will automatically connect you to an online printing service appropriate to your current location.

**2** Click on the Create button to access options for creating items such as photo books, card and calendars. These are done with online services

# Playing a Music CD

Music is one of the areas that has revived Apple's fortunes in recent years, primarily through the iPod music player and iTunes; and also the iTunes music store, where music can be bought online. iTunes is a versatile program but its basic function is to play a music CD. To do this:

**Don't forget**

iTunes can be accessed by clicking on this icon on the Dock.

**Beware**

Never import music and use it for commercial purposes as this would be a breach of copyright.

**1** Insert the CD in the CD/DVD drive

**2** By default, iTunes will open and display this window. Click No if you just want to play the CD

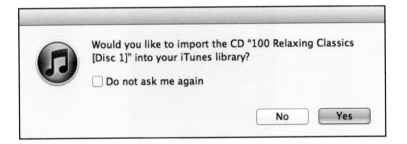

Would you like to import the CD "100 Relaxing Classics [Disc 1]" into your iTunes library?

☐ Do not ask me again

No   Yes

**3** Click on the CD name

DEVICES

● 100 Relaxing Classics... ⏏

**4** Click on this button to play the whole CD

**5** Click on this button if you want to copy the music from the CD onto your hard drive

Import CD

# Organizing Your Music

iTunes offers great flexibility when it comes to organizing
your music.

 Click here to view all of the
music in your iTunes library

 Click on this button to display a quick
view of your iTunes music

| √ Name | Time | Artist | ▲ Album |
|---|---|---|---|
| √ Digital Booklet – The Suburbs | | Arcade Fire | The Suburbs |
| √ The Suburbs | 5:15 | Arcade Fire | The Suburbs |
| √ Ready to Start | 4:16 | Arcade Fire | The Suburbs |
| √ Modern Man | 4:40 | Arcade Fire | The Suburbs |
| √ Rococo | 3:57 | Arcade Fire | The Suburbs |
| √ Empty Room | 2:52 | Arcade Fire | The Suburbs |
| √ City With No Children | 3:12 | Arcade Fire | The Suburbs |
| √ Half Light I | 4:14 | Arcade Fire | The Suburbs |

Click on this button to view your iTunes
library according to the relevant covers for
the music

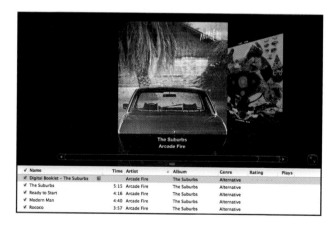

Click on this button to play all of
the music in your iTunes library in a
random order

...cont'd

## Adding a playlist

A playlist in iTunes is a selection of music that you want to group together under certain headings, such as for a party or a certain mood or genre. To create a playlist:

**1** Click on this button at the bottom of the Library section panel

**2** Enter a name for the new playlist

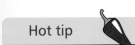
**3** Click on the required items of music in the main window

| ▲ | √ | Name |
|---|---|---|
| 1 ⊘ | √ | Vivaldi: Violin Concerto In E, O... ○ |
| 2 ⊘ | √ | Andante 2nd Mvt Brandenburg... ○ |
| 3 ⊘ | √ | Largo 2nd Mvt Concerto Gross... ○ |
| 4 ⊘ | √ | Beethoven: Bagatelles, Op. 11... ○ |
| 5 ⊘ | √ | Mozart: Horn Concerto #4 In E Fl... |

**4** Drag the selected items over the playlist folder and release

**5** The selected items are included in the playlist

# Downloading Music

As well as playing music, iTunes can also be used to legally download music, via the iTunes Store. This contains a huge range of music and you have to register on the site once. After this you can download music for use on your Mac and also for downloading onto an iPod. To do this:

**1** Under the Library section in iTunes, click on the iTunes Store button

**2** The iTunes store offers music, videos, television programs, audiobooks and podcasts for downloading

Beware

Never use illegal music download sites. Apart from the legal factor, they are much more likely to contain viruses and spyware.

**3** Look for items in the iTunes store either by browsing through the sections of the site, or enter a keyword in the search box at the top of the window

## ...cont'd

**4** Locate an item you want to buy

Music > Alternative > Mumford & Sons

**Sigh No More**

iTunes Review

Freak folk introduced a ne
Candle and of course Fair
songs, performed and rec

**5** Click on the Buy button (at this point you will have to register with the iTunes Store, if you have not already done so)

**Buy Album**

**6** Once you have registered, you will have to enter a username and password to complete your purchase

Sign In to download from the iTunes Store
If you have an Apple Account, enter your Apple ID and password. Otherwise, if you are an AOL member, enter your AOL screen name and password.

Apple ID:
nickvandome@mac.com    Example: steve@me.com
Password:

AOL.                                Forgot Password?
☐ Remember password

(?) Create New Account                    Cancel    Buy

**7** Once the item has been downloaded it is available through iTunes on your Mac, under the Purchased button

STORE
📑 iTunes Store
⊂Q Ping
⊒♪ Purchased

# Adding an iPod

Since their introduction in 2001 iPods have become an inescapable part of modern life. It is impossible to sit on a bus or a train without seeing someone with the ubiquitous white earbuds, humming away to their favorite tunes. iPods are for everyone and they should not be seen as the preserve of the young – although they may select a slightly different type of music to play on them. iPods are designed to work seamlessly with iTunes and the latter can be used to load music onto the former. To do this:

1. Connect your iPod to the Mac with the supplied USB or Firewire cable

2. iTunes will open automatically and display details about the attached iPod

3. iTunes should automatically start copying music from the iTunes Library onto the iPod.
If not, select the iPod under the Devices heading

4. Select File>Sync from the iTunes Menu bar to synchronize iTunes and your iPod

# Earbuds and Headphones

When listening to music there will probably be occasions when you will want to use either earbuds or headphones to save other people from hearing your music. The choice between the two could have a significant impact on your overall audio experience and comfort.

### Earbuds

These are essentially small plastic buds that fit inside the ear. The most common example are the ones supplied with iPods. While these are small and convenient, they do not usually offer the best sound quality and, perhaps more importantly for some people, they can be uncomfortable to use, particularly for prolonged periods.

**Beware**

It is worth investing in good quality earbuds or headphones otherwise the escape of sound could annoy people around you.

### Headphones

These go over the ears rather than in them and are generally more comfortable as a result. It is worth investing in a good set of headphones because the sound quality will ensure that it is money well spent. The one downside of headphones is that they can be slightly bulky, but some are designed so that they fold away into a small, compact pouch.

# Creating Music

For those who are as interested in creating music as listening to it, GarageBand can be used for this very purpose. It can take a bit of time and practice to become fully proficient with GarageBand but it is worth persevering with if you are musically inclined and want to compose your own. To use GarageBand:

1. Click on this icon on the Dock

2. Click on the New Project button

3. Give your new project a name and select a instrument with which to create it

4. Click on this button to start recording

5. Click on the keyboard to record the music

85

**Don't forget**

GarageBand can appear quite complex at first and it takes a little bit of time to feel comfortable with it.

## ...cont'd

6 Click on this button to view a library of music loops which can be included in your song

7 A list of pre-recorded music loops is displayed

8 Select a style and an instrument. The available loops are displayed underneath the Name tab

9 Select a loop and drag it onto the timeline to add it to your song

10 The completed song is shown in the timeline. This can consist of several separate tracks

# Listening to the Radio

For the radio lover, iTunes offers literally hundreds of digital radio stations. To access these:

**1** Under the Library section in iTunes, click on the Radio button

**2** Select a category

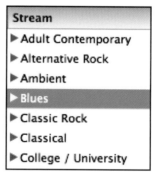

**3** Select a station from the required category. Double-click on it to access the station

**4** The station currently playing is shown at the top of the iTunes window

# Creating a Home Movie

For home movie buffs, iMovie offers options for downloading, editing and publishing your efforts:

**1** Click on this button on the Dock

**2** Attach a digital video camera to your Mac with a Firewire cable

**3** Click here to access the camera

**4** Click here to play the video in the camera

**5** Click on the Capture button to copy the video into iMovie

**6** Click on the Done button to return to the editing environment

**7** Downloaded video clips are shown here

**8** Drag a clip into the Project Library window to add it to a new video project

**Don't forget**

Video clips can be edited by selecting them in the project window and then clicking on the Clip Trimmer option at the bottom left of the clip. The clip can then be trimmed by dragging the beginning or the end of the clip.

**9**   Click on this button to access Transition options

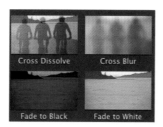

**10**   Click on this button to access Text options

**11**   Click on this button to access Sound options

**12**   Text, transitions and sound can be added to a movie by dragging them between the video clips

**13**   Click Share on the Menu bar and select an option for exporting the finished movie

# Sharing a Home Movie

Once video has been created, it can be shared between family and friends on a DVD. This can be done through the iDVD program. To do this:

1. Click on this icon on the Dock

2. Click on the Create a New Project option

3. Give the project a name

4. Click on the Create button

5. Click on the Themes button

6. Double-click on a theme to select it as the background of your DVD

**7**  Click on the Media button **Media**

**8**  Click on the Photos tab **Photos**

**9**  Select a photo and drag it onto the Drop Zones of the theme

**Don't forget**

If Drop Zones are left empty a warning will appear when you try and burn the final DVD. However, this can be ignored.

**91**

**10**  Click on the Movies tab **Movies**

**11**  Select a movie and drag it onto the Theme

...cont'd

**12** Click on the movie name and type a new name if required

**13** Click on the Audio tab

Audio

**14** Select an audio element that you want to use as background music for the DVD and drag it onto the Theme

| Audio | Photos | Movies |
|---|---|---|

▶ 🎸 GarageBand

▼ 🎵 iTunes

🎵 Music

🎬 Movies

🎙 Podcasts

📖 Books

🎵 Purchased

| Name | Artist | Time |
|---|---|---|
| 🎵 The Suburbs | Arcade Fire | 5:15 |
| 🎵 Ready to Start | Arcade Fire | 4:15 |
| 🎵 Modern Man | Arcade Fire | 4:39 |
| 🎵 Rococo | Arcade Fire | 3:56 |
| 🎵 Empty Room | Arcade Fire | 2:51 |
| 🎵 City With No Children | Arcade Fire | 3:11 |

**15** Click on this button to edit the Drop Zone

**Don't forget**

Drop zones can be edited by adding different photos.

**16** Click on this button to view the animation of the Theme

**17** Click on this button to preview the project

**Hot tip**

Burn DVDs at a slower speed than the maximum available. This will ensure a better chance of it being burned correctly.

**18** Click on this button to burn the finished DVD

# Playing Chess

Game playing relaxation is not ignored on the Mac and many hours can be spent playing chess against the computer. To do this:

**1** In Finder, click on the Applications button or access the Launchpad

**2** Double-click on the Chess icon

**3** By default you are white and the computer is black

**4** Move your pieces by clicking on them and dragging them to the required square

**5** Once you have moved, Black will move automatically

**Don't forget**

In the Chess application it is possible to play against the computer or another person. This can be specified when you select Game>New to start a new game.

# 5 At Home

This chapter reveals options for getting productive and creative on your Mac, creating letters, household budgets and presentations.

# Productivity Options

As well as using Macs for leisure and entertainment activities, they are also ideally suited for more functional purposes such as creating letters and documents, doing household expenses and creating posters or presentations. As always in the world of technology there is more than one option about which program to use when performing these tasks. Some of these include:

### iWork

This is an Apple program that is designed specifically for the Mac. It contains a suite of productivity programs including those for word processing, spreadsheets and presentations. Although not as well known as the more ubiquitous Microsoft Office suite of programs, iWork is an easy to use and a powerful option that will fulfil the productivity needs of most users. The iWork programs are Pages, Numbers and Keynote and they can all be bought from the App Store.

Where applicable, the productivity examples in this chapter use iWork.

### Microsoft Office

Even in the world of Macs it is impossible to avoid the software giant that is Microsoft. For users of Microsoft Office (the suite of programs containing the likes of Word, Excel, Powerpoint) the good news is that there is a version written specifically for the Mac. This works in the same way as the IBM-compatible PC version and for anyone who has used it before the Mac version will look reassuringly familiar. However, on the downside, Office is relatively expensive and the programs contain a lot of functionality that most users will never need.

### TextEdit

For anyone who just wants to do some fairly basic word processing, the built-in Mac app TextEdit is an option. This can be used to create letters and other similar documents. However, it does not have the versatility of either iWork or Microsoft Office.

**Hot tip**

Files in both iWork and Microsoft Office for the Mac can easily be saved for use on a Windows PC.
To do this, select the required file format in the Save window.

# Accessing a Dictionary

A good starting point for any productivity function is a dictionary. On the Mac you do not have to worry about having a large book to hand as there are two options that cover this task.

## Applications dictionary

Within the Applications folder there is a fully functioning dictionary. To use this:

**1** In Finder, click on the Applications button or access the Launchpad

**2** Double-click on the Dictionary icon

**3** Select the option you want to use for looking up a word

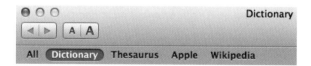

**4** In the search box, type in the word you want to look up

**5** The results are displayed in the dictionary window

...cont'd

### Dashboard dictionary

The Dashboard is an app within Mac OS X that offers a number of widgets, or small programs, for a variety of useful tasks such as weather reports, maps, a clock and a calculator. It also has a dictionary. To use this:

**1** Click on this icon on the Dock to access the Dashboard widgets

**2** If the Dictionary widget is not showing click on this button to view the available widgets

**3** Click on the Dictionary widget to add it to the main Dashboard (which appears above the Desktop)

**4** The Dictionary widget can be used in a similar way to the one on the previous page

# Creating a Letter

One of the most common word processing tasks is writing a letter and it is something that most of us have to do for either business or pleasure. This could be a letter to a family member or a letter of complaint. Whatever the subject matter it is worth making your letters look as professional, or as stylish, as possible. To create a letter in Pages:

**1**  In Finder, click on the Applications button or access the Launchpad

**2**  Click on the Pages icon

Don't forget

There are enough different letter templates in Pages for you not to need to create your own. If required, existing ones can be amended.

**3**  In the template window, click on the Letters option

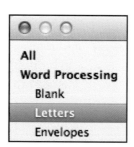

**4**  Click on a style for the type of letter you want to create

**5**  Click on the Choose button

6 An untitled letter is displayed based on the template you have selected

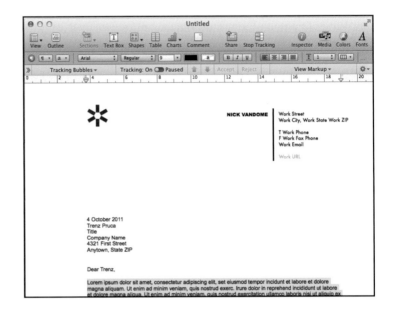

7 Double-click on an element of the letter and overtype to change it

8 Click once in the draft text of the letter. This will highlight all of the text

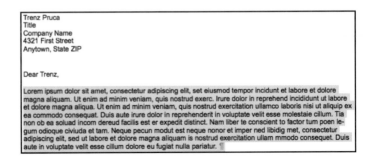

**9** Write your own text for the letter

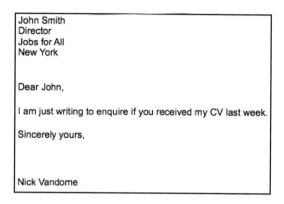

**10** Select File>Save... from the Menu bar

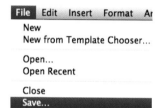

**11** Browse to the folder into which you want to save the letter

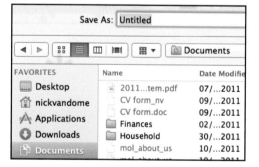

**12** Give the letter a name

Save As: work_enquiry

**13** Click on the Save button

# Formatting a Newsletter

Newsletters are not just the preserve of the business world: they are a great source of information for local clubs, communities and also for family updates. To create and format a newsletter in Pages:

1  In Finder, click on the Applications button or access the Launchpad

2  Click on the Pages icon

3  In the Template Chooser window, click on the Newsletters option

4  Click on a style for the type of newsletter you want to create

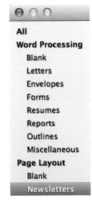

5  Click on the Choose button

**6** Click on a text element to select it

*the* **SMITH** *family*

**7** Overtype the selection with your own text

*the* **VANDOMES**

**8** Click on an image placeholder (this is just a default image that can be changed with your own photos)

### Hot tip

When an element is selected it is highlighted by a box with small markers around its perimeter. By dragging these markers you can resize the item.

**9** Click on the Media button on the toolbar

Media

...cont'd

10 In the Media window browse to the photo you want to use

11 Drag the selected photo onto the placeholder

12 If required, you can drag the image around the page to re-position it

**13** Click on the Pages button on the toolbar to add new pages to the newsletter

Pages

**14** Click on the type of new page you want to include

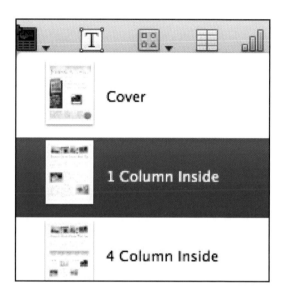

Cover

1 Column Inside

4 Column Inside

Include plenty of photos in your newsletter to make it visually appealing.

**15** Format the new page in the same way as the cover page

*Vandome Family Vacation*

**16** Save the newsletter in the same way as a letter

# Using a Calculator

Financial matters can sometimes be a chore but they are a necessary part of life, whether it is working out household expenses or calculating available spending money. Even for the best mathematicians a calculator is a trusty friend when it comes to arithmetic. Luckily the Mac has one ready-made:

**1** In Finder, click on the Applications button or access the Launchpad

**2** Double-click on the Calculator icon

**3** Click on the calculator's buttons to perform calculations

**Don't forget**

If you are going to be doing anything more than basic calculations, the scientific option may be more useful than the basic one.

**4** Select View from the Menu bar and select an option for the type of calculator being displayed

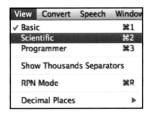

**5** The option selected in Step 4 is now available

# Doing Household Accounts

As well as being useful for word processing iWork can also be used for financial accounting, such as keeping track of the household accounts. To do this:

**1** In Finder, click on the Applications button or access the Launchpad

**2** Double-click on the Numbers icon

**3** Select File>New from Template Chooser

**4** In the template window click on the Personal Finance button

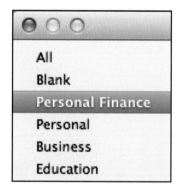

107

**5** Select the Budget template

**6** Click on the Choose button

## ...cont'd

**7** The budget template is displayed. All of the items can be edited with your own information

| Monthly Net Income | |
| --- | --- |
| Income Type | Amount |
| Monthly Net Income | £4,500 |
| Other Monthly Income | £2,500 |
| Available Cash | £7,000 |

| Additional Income | | |
| --- | --- | --- |
| Details | Month | Amount |
| Mid Year Bonus | June | £2,000 |
| Year End Bonus | December | £3,000 |
| | January | |
| Total Additional Income | | £5,000 |

| Monthly Expenses | |
| --- | --- |
| Expense | Costs |
| Mortgage | £2,300 |
| Taxes | £600 |
| Car Payment | £350 |
| Car Insurance | £60 |
| Home Owners Insurance | £127 |
| Cable Bill | £120 |
| Gas/Electric | £88 |
| Monthly Prescription | £50 |
| Total Monthly Expenses | £3,695 |

| Planned Expenses | | |
| --- | --- | --- |
| Expenditure | Month | Amount |
| November vacation | November | £450 |
| Home for the holidays | December | £600 |
| Gifts for family | December | £300 |
| Family vacation | July | £880 |
| | January | |
| | January | |
| | January | |
| | January | |
| Total Planned Expenses | | £2,230 |

**8** Click on a style to change the formatting of the displayed budget

**9** Click on one of the budget topics

**10** The selected element is highlighted

| Monthly Expenses | |
| --- | --- |
| Expense | Costs |
| Mortgage | £2,300 |
| Taxes | £600 |
| Car Payment | £350 |
| Car Insurance | £60 |
| Home Owners Insurance | £127 |
| Cable Bill | £120 |
| Gas/Electric | £88 |
| Monthly Prescription | £50 |
| Total Monthly Expenses | £3,695 |

11 Double-click on an individual item to select it

4    **Car Payment**

12 Overtype the selected item with your own details

4    **Motor Home Payment**

13 Select a cell containing
financial information. Edit the
information, as required

£120

£88

£50

£3,695

14 Linked cells are updated
accordingly

£300

£88

£50

£3,875

15 Save the spreadsheet in the same way as for a letter
or a newsletter

**Don't forget**

Linked cells are
controlled by a
mathematical equation
that ensures that if
one is updated then
the data in the linked
cell changes too.

# Creating a Presentation

Presentations are a great way to produce customized slideshows of family photographs or promote activities in local clubs or charities. To do this in iWork:

**1** In Finder, click on the Applications button or access the Launchpad

**2** Click on the keynote icon

**3** Select File>New from Template Chooser

**4** Click on a type of presentation

**5** Click on the Choose button

**6** Double-click on the text to select it

# My Slideshow

## Double-click to edit

**7** Overtype with your own text

**8** Click on the Media button on the Menu bar

**9** Browse to your photos

**Beware**

When adding text to a presentation, make sure that it is not too small and that there is not too much of it.

111

**10** Drag a selected photo onto the placeholder photo on the slide. This replaces the placeholder photo with your own

11 To add more text to a slide, click on the Text Box button on the Menu bar

12 Drag the text tool on the slide to create a text box and type the required text

13 Click on these buttons for options for formatting the color and type of the text

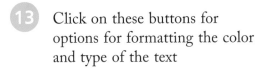

14 To add more slides click on the New button on the Menu bar. Add content in the same way as the original slide

15 Click on the Play button on the Menu bar to preview the presentation

16 Save the presentation in the same way as a letter, a newsletter or a spreadsheet

# 6 Getting Online

*Accessing the Internet and World Wide Web (WWW) is essential for most computer users. This chapter shows you how to use your Mac to start browsing the Web.*

# Accessing the Internet

Access to the Internet is an accepted part of the computing world and it is unusual for users not to want to do this. Not only does this provide a gateway to the World Wide Web but also email.

Connecting to the Internet with a Mac is done through the System Preferences. To do this:

1  Click on the System Preferences icon on the Dock

2  Click on the Network icon

3  Check that your method of connecting to the Internet is active i.e. colored green

4  Click on the Assist Me... button to access wizards for connecting to the Internet with your preferred method of connection

# Around the Web

When you are surfing the Web it is important to feel comfortable with both your browser and also the websites at which you are looking. Most websites are a collection of linked pages that you can move between by clicking on links (also known as hyperlinks) that connect the different pages.

### Address bar

The Address bar is the box at the top of the browser that displays the address of the web page that is currently being displayed. Each web page has a unique address so the address changes whenever you move to a different page. The Address bar displays the web page address in this format:

### Main content

The full content of a web page is displayed in the main browser window:

Don't forget

Macs have a built-in Web browser known as Safari. This can be accessed from the Dock by clicking on this icon:

...cont'd

**Hot tip**

The Toolbar contains a homepage button which takes you to your own homepage i.e. the page that is accessed when you first open up your browser.

### Toolbar

This is a collection of icons at the top of the browser that has various options for navigating around web pages and accessing options such as newsfeeds and printing pages:

### Menu bar

This contains various menus with options for navigating around, and customizing web pages. In Safari it is located at the top of the Safari window:

**Safari**    File    Edit    View    History    Bookmarks    Window    Help

### Navigation bars

These are groups of buttons that appear on websites to help users navigate within the site. Generally, the main navigation bars appear in the same place on every page of the site:

**home**    **books**    **corporate information**    **resource center**

**Don't forget**

The items that make up the navigation bar are buttons, or textual links, that take you to another location within the site.

### Search box

Most websites have a search box, into which keywords or phrases can be entered to search over the whole site:

Vandome    go

## Links

This is the device that is used to move between pages within a website, or from one website to another. Links can be in a variety of styles, but most frequently they are in the form of buttons, underlined text or a roll-over (i.e. a button or piece of text that changes appearance when the cursor is passed over it):

The cursor usually turns into a pointing hand when it is over a link on a website.

**terms of use : privacy policy : write for us : accessibility**

## Tabs

Safari has an option for using different tabs. This enables you to open different web pages within the same browser window. You can then move between the pages by clicking on each tab, at the top of the window:

## Bookmarks

Everyone has their favorite web pages that they return to again and again. These can be added to a list in a browser so that they can be accessed quickly when required. There is usually a button at the top of the browser that can add the current page to the list of bookmarked items:

History **Bookmarks** Window Help

117

# Setting a Homepage

A homepage is what a browser opens by default whenever it is first launched. This is usually a page associated with the company that created the browser i.e. the Apple homepage for Safari. However, it is possible to customize the browser so that it opens with your own choice of homepage. To do this in Safari:

**1** Open Safari and click on Safari>Preferences... from the Menu bar

**2** Click on the General tab

**3** Click on the Set to Current Page if you want the current page you are viewing to be your homepage

**Set to Current Page**

**4** Enter a web address in the Home page box to set this as your homepage

Homepage: http://www.apple.com/

**5** Click on this button to close the Preferences window

# Using Tabs

Safari was one of the first browsers to use tabs and this is still an integral part of its function.

### Adding tabs
To add new tabs in Safari:

**1** Select File>New Tab from the Menu bar

**2** The new tab offers pages from your Top Sites. Select one of these or enter a new web address

**Don't forget**

Tabs are usually a better option than opening a lot of different browser windows, as it keeps each new page within the same window.

119

**3** Browse in the normal way in the new tab (the content in any other open tabs remains untouched)

**4** To access, and change, shortcut keys for creating and using

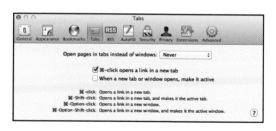

tabs, click on Safari>Preferences from the Menu bar and select the Tabs tab

# Searching the Web

With the vast number of items on the Web it is essential to have a good search facility close at hand at all times.
In Safari there is a Google search box built in to the toolbar.
To use this:

**1** The Google search box is located here

**2** Type the required search keyword(s) and press Enter

**3** The search results are displayed in the main browser window. Click on one to view that page

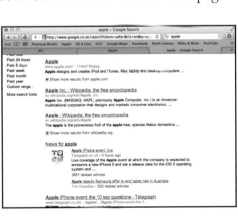

# Adding Bookmarks

Bookmarks in Safari are favorite pages to which you want to have regular, and fast, access. Bookmarks can be added to a bar at the top of the Safari window or a menu that is accessed from the Safari Menu bar.

### Bookmarks Bar

To bookmark pages to the Bookmarks Bar:

**1** Navigate to the page on the Web you want to bookmark

**2** Click on this button on the Safari toolbar

**3** Enter a name for the bookmarked page

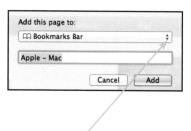

**4** Click here and select Bookmarks Bar

**5** Click on the Add button

**6** The page is added to the Bookmarks Bar. If it is not visible, select View>Show Bookmarks Bar from the Safari Menu bar. Click on a bookmark to move to that site

...cont'd

### Bookmarks Menu

To bookmark pages to the Bookmarks Menu:

**1** Navigate to the page on the Web you want to bookmark

**2** Click on this button on the Safari toolbar

**3** Enter a name for the bookmarked page

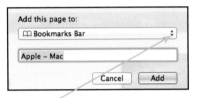

**4** Click here and select Bookmarks Menu option

**5** Click on the Add button

**6** To view the Bookmarks Menu, select Bookmarks from the Menu bar

**7** Click on the Add Bookmark Folder link if you want to create folders into which you can place your bookmarks, according to subject

# Viewing Your Online History

In any Web session it is possible to look at dozens, or hundreds, of websites and pages. To make it easier to retrace your steps and return to previously viewed pages, the History option in Safari can be used. To do this:

1. Select History from the Safari Menu bar

2. Click on an item here to return to a page that has been viewed in your current browsing session

3. Click on a date to view items that have been accessed previously

> Sunday, 2 October 2011
> Saturday, 1 October 2011
> Friday, 30 September 2011
> Wednesday, 28 September 2011

4. Click on Clear History to remove all of the items in your browsing history

> Wednesday, 21 September 2011
>
> Clear History...

123

# Safari Reader

Web pages can be complex and cluttered things at times. On occasions you may want to just read the content of one story on a web page without all of the extra material in view. In Safari this can be done with the Reader function. To do this:

**Beware**

Not all web pages support the Reader functionality in Safari.

**1** Select View>Show Reader from

| View | History | Bookm |
|---|---|---|
| Hide Toolbar | | |
| Customize Toolbar... | | |
| Hide Bookmarks Bar | | |
| Show Tab Bar | | |
| Show Status Bar | | |
| **Show Reader** | | |

the Safari menu bar

**2** Click on the Reader button in the address bar of a web page that supports this functionality

**3** The button turns purple once the Reader is activated

Reader

**4** The content is displayed in a text format, with any photos from the original

Defiant Gaddafi 'vows to fight'

24 August 2011 Last updated at 09:33

The BBC's Rupert Wingfield-Hayes in Tripoli: "The city erupted in gunfire"

Col Muammar Gaddafi has made a speech vowing death or victory in the fight against "aggression", after Libyan rebels seized his Tripoli compound.

In the audio speech, the colonel, whose whereabouts remain unknown, said he had made a "tactical" retreat from his Bab al-Aziziya compound in the capital.

**Don't forget**

If RSS is showing in the address bar, click on this to show RSS newsfeeds for that site. These are textual newsfeeds that update automatically when there are new items.

**5** Click on this button on the Safari toolbar if you want to save a page to read at a later date

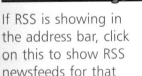

**6** Click on this button to add the page

Add Page

# Being Interactive Online

*This chapter shows some of the activities that can be undertaken on the Web. It covers buying items from online shops, delving into your family history and playing online games.*

# Shopping Online

The Web is a lot more than just a means of discovering facts and figures. It is also a means of doing business in terms of buying and selling. This can be for small or large purchases, but either way, online shopping has revolutionized our retail lives.

When you are shopping online there are some guidelines that should be followed to try and ensure you are in a safe online environment and do not spend too much money:

- Make a note of what you want to buy and stick to this once you have found it. Online shopping sites are adept at displaying a lot of enticing offers and it is a lot easier to buy something by clicking a button than it is to physically take it to a checkout

- Never buy anything that is promoted to you via an email, unless it is from a company who you have asked to send you promotional information

- When paying for items, make sure that the online site has a secure area for accepting payment and credit card details. A lot of sites display information about this within their payment area and another way to ascertain this is to check in the Address bar of the payment page. If it is within a secure area the address of the page will start with "https" rather than the standard "http"

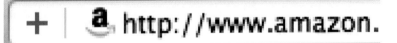

## Using online shopping

The majority of online shopping sites are similar in their operation:

- Goods are identified

- Goods are placed in a shopping basket

- Once the shopping is completed you proceed to the checkout

- You enter your shipping details and pay for the goods, usually with a credit card

On some sites you have to register before you can buy goods and in some cases this enables you to perform your shopping quicker by using a 1-click system. This means that all of your billing and payment details are already stored on the site and you can buy goods simply by clicking one button without having to re-enter your details. One of the most prominent sites to use this method is Amazon:

**Beware**

Be careful when shopping online as you can quickly get carried away since making purchases can be so easy.

127

# Booking a Vacation

Just as a lot of retailers have been creating an online presence, the same is also true for vacation companies and travel agents. It is now possible to book almost any type of vacation on the Web, from cruises to city breaks.

Several sites offer full travel services where they can deal with flights, hotels, insurance, car hire and excursions. These sites include:

- Expedia at www.expedia.com

- Travelocity at www.travelocity.com

- Tripadvisor at www.tripadvisor.com

These sites usually list special offers and last minute deals on their homepages and there is also a facility for specifying your precise requirements. To do this:

**128**

1　Select your vacation requirements

2　Enter flight details (if applicable)

3　Enter dates for your vacation

4　Click on the Search button

In addition to sites that do everything for you it is also possible to book your vacation on individual sites. This can be particularly useful for cruises and also for booking hotels around the world. Some websites to look at are:

## Cruises

- Cruises.com at www.cruises.com

- Carnival at www.carnival.com

- Princess Cruises at www.princess.com

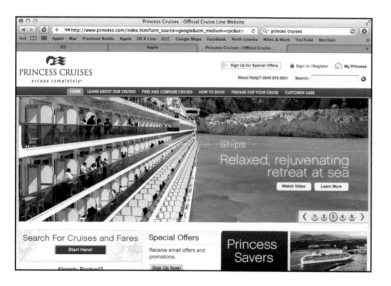

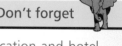

**Don't forget**

Vacation and hotel websites usually have versions that are specific to the geographical location in which you are situated.

## Hotels

- Hotels.com at www.hotels.com

- Late Rooms at www.laterooms.com

- Choice Hotels International at www.choicehotels.com

# Researching Family History

A recent growth industry on the Web has been family history, or genealogy. Hundreds of organizations around the world have now digitized their records concerning individuals and family histories and there are numerous websites that provide online access to these records. Some of these sites are:

- Ancestry at www.ancestry.com

- Genealogy.com at www.genealogy.com

- Familysearch at www.familysearch.org

- RootsWeb.com at www.rootsweb.com

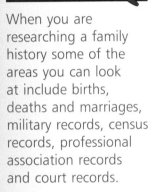
**130**

Most genealogy sites require you to register, for a fee, before you can conduct extensive family research on their sites, but once you do the process is similar on them all:

1  Enter the details of the family members in the search boxes

2  Click on the Get started button

3  The results are displayed for the names searched against

**Don't forget**

Some sites offer a free initial search, but after that you will have to pay for each search.

131

4  Click on the Search for Records button to get a detailed report for your information. This may require registering on the site

5  On some sites there is a facility for creating your family tree. Enter the relevant details

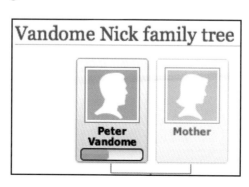

# Price Comparison Sites

Everyone likes to get value for money when shopping or, better still, a bargain. On the Web it is possible to try and find the best possible prices for items before you buy them. This is done through price comparison sites that show the prices for items from a range of online retailers. Some of the price comparison sites include:

- PriceGrabber at www.pricegrabber.com

- PriceRunner at www.pricerunner.com

- Pricewatch at www.pricewatch.com

To use a price comparison site:

**1** Select one of the online price comparison sites

**2** Select a category for the type of product you want to buy

> **Sound & Vision**
> All TVs, LCD TVs, LED TVs, Plasma TVs, 3D TVs, MP3 Players, Phones, Mobile Phones

**3** Locate the product you want to buy

Samsung UE46D7000 - Compare prices

46 in, 3D-Ready LED, HDTV 1080p, Samsung

Product rating: ☆☆☆☆☆
Price range: £ 1,394.95 - £ 1,699.99

**4** Click on the Compare Prices link or tab

**5** The available retailers and their prices are displayed

**6** Click on a retailer's link or icon to go to their site, from where the item can be purchased

**Beware**

Just because certain items are displayed on a price comparison site does not mean that you cannot get them cheaper elsewhere.

133

# Shopping on eBay

eBay is one of the phenomena of the online world. Started as a small site in California it has grown into a multi-billion business with online auctions and also standard online retailer transactions. To buy and sell items on eBay you have to be registered. This can be done from the eBay homepage by clicking on the Register button or link. This takes you through the registration process, which is free.

### Buying items

Once you have registered you can start buying and selling items. In some ways it is better to start by buying some cheaper items just to get used to the system. To do this:

**Beware**

Most people are honest on eBay but you do sometimes get unscrupulous buyers and sellers.

**134**

1 To find items to buy, enter a keyword in the search box and click on the Search button, or

> **stamps**
>
> **Search**

2 Click on the Categories button and drill down through the various categories

> ✓ All Categories
> Antiques
> Art
> Baby
> Books
> Business & Industrial
> Cameras & Photo
> Cars, Boats, Vehicles & Parts
> Cell Phones & PDAs
> Clothing, Shoes & Accessories
> Coins & Paper Money
> Collectibles
> Computers & Networking
> Consumer Electronics
> Crafts
> Dolls & Bears
> DVDs & Movies

3 When you find items in which you are interested, select whether you want to view them according to Auctions, Buy It Now (single price purchase) or both

> | All items | Auctions only | Buy It Now |

4 Click on an item to view its details

5 For Buy It Now items, click on this button to purchase the item

6 For auction items, enter a bid in the Place Bid box and click on the Place Bid button

7 Review the item and purchase details

**Don't forget**

Once you have completed the transaction you can leave feedback about the seller.

8 If you want to proceed with your bid, click on the Confirm bid button

9 If you are successful in the auction you will be notified on eBay and also via email. At this point you pay the vendor for the item and they should mail it to you

## Selling items

If you want to sell items on eBay you have to first list them for sale. To do this:

1. Click on the Sell button at the top of the eBay window

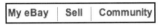

2. Click on the List your item button

List your item

3. Enter the keywords for your item and click on the Start selling button

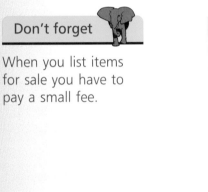
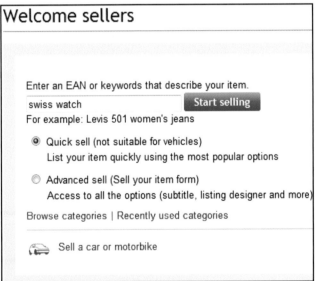

# Welcome sellers

Enter an EAN or keywords that describe your item.

swiss watch    **Start selling**

For example: Levis 501 women's jeans

◉ Quick sell (not suitable for vehicles)
List your item quickly using the most popular options

○ Advanced sell (Sell your item form)
Access to all the options (subtitle, listing designer and more)

Browse categories | Recently used categories

🚗 Sell a car or motorbike

4. Complete the wizard for selling items. This includes a detailed description of the item and photographs

5. Once the wizard has been completed the item will be listed in the relevant category on eBay

# Online Finances

## Online banking

Online banking has helped to transform our financial activities in the same way as online shopping has transformed our retail ones. Most major banks have online banking facilities and they can be used for a number of services, including:

- Managing your accounts

- Transferring money

- Paying bills

- Applying for credit cards

- Paying credit cards

- Applying for loans

Before you can use any of these online services you have to first register and apply for an online account:

**Don't forget**

Online banking is generally as secure as any other form of banking transaction and it has the advantage that you can check your accounts as frequently as you like.

**1** On the homepage of most bank websites there are boxes for signing in if you are an existing online customer or applying for a new account. Select the relevant option and you will then be taken through the necessary steps

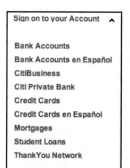

...cont'd

### Stocks and shares online

An extension of online banking is being able to deal in stocks and shares on the Web. You can buy and sell on the stock market without having to leave the comfort of your own home. A number of financial services websites offer this facility and they also provide a lot of background information as well as the buying and selling function. If you are going to be trading stocks and shares on the Web it is a good idea to find out as much about them before you start trading. In this respect the websites of relevant stock markets provide a very useful source of information:

**Beware**

Never buy stocks and shares from any offers you receive by email.

**1** Enter details to get current stock prices

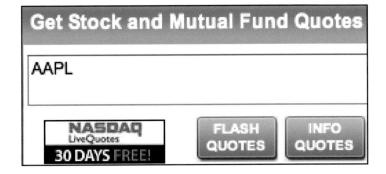

**2** Use the Research areas to find out the history and performance of individual stocks and shares

**Quotes & Research**

**3** Check the latest News section for updates

**News & Commentary**

# Maps Online

Maps have fascinated mankind for thousands of years and with the Web it has never been easier to view local, national or international maps. In addition, the sites that provide these services also provide a host of additional information about hotels, airports, schools and civic amenities. Two sites to look at for maps are:

- Multimap at www. multimap.com

- Google Maps at http://maps.google.com

To use an online mapping service:

1. Enter a name or zip code of somewhere you want to look up

**Colorado, United States**

2. The results display the required map

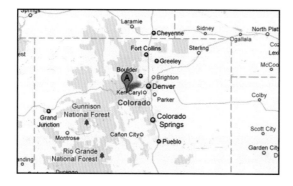

3. Use this slider to zoom in or out of the map

**Don't forget**

Multimap now appears under the Bing website, but it can still be accessed with the Multimap address.

**Don't forget**

Online mapping services can also provide directions between two different locations.

# Online Games

Online gambling has developed in some countries in recent years but it is also possible to play online games, such as bridge and backgammon, without the need to gamble away your life savings. Although some of these sites do allow you to play for money, others offer a less financially pressurized environment. For both bridge and backgammon sites you can either play against the computer or other people who are on the site. Either way, you are usually presented with a graphic interface of the action:

**Don't forget**

Sites for online bridge or backgammon can be found by entering these keywords into the Google search box.

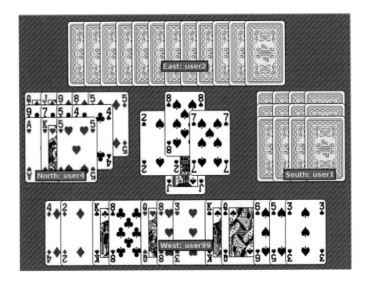

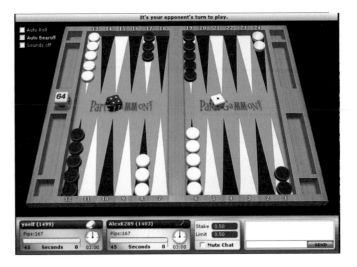

# 8 Keeping in Touch

*Communication, as much as money, makes the world go round. This chapter shows how to use the Mac tools to communicate, interact and share by email, text and video.*

# Setting up Email

Email is an essential element for most computer users and Macs come with their own email program called Mail. This covers all of the email functionality that anyone could need.

When first using Mail you have to set up your email account. This information will be available from the company who provides your email service, although in some cases Mail may obtain this information automatically. To view your Mail account details:

**1**  Click on this icon on the Dock

**2**  Select Mail>Preferences... from the Menu bar

**3**  Click on the Accounts tab

**4**  If it has not already been included, enter the details of your email account in the Account Information section

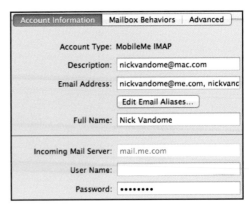

**5**  Click on this button to close the Mail Preferences window

# Adding Mailboxes

Before you start creating email messages it is a good idea to create a folder structure (mailboxes) for your emails. This will allow you to sort your emails into relevant subjects when you receive them, rather than having all of them sitting in your Inbox. To add new mailboxes:

**1** Mailboxes are displayed in the Mailboxes panel

**2** At the bottom of the Mailboxes panel, click on this icon

**3** Select where you want the mailbox to be created (by default this will be On My Mac)

**4** Enter a name for the new mailbox

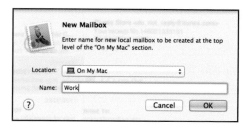

**5** Click on the OK button

**6** The new mailbox is added to the current list

**Don't forget**

Different mailboxes can be used to store emails according to their subject matter.

# Creating Email

Mail enables you to send and receive emails and also format them to your own style. This can be simply formatting text or adding customized stationery. To use Mail:

**1** Click on the Get Mail button to download available email messages

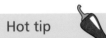
**2** Click on the New Message button to create a new email

**3** Enter a recipient in the To box, a title in the Subject box and then text for the email in the main window

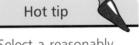
**4** Click on the Format button to access options for formatting the text in the email

**5** Click on these buttons to Reply to, Reply to All or Forward an email you have received

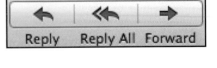

**6** Select or open an email and click on the Delete button to remove it

# Email Conversations

Within Mail you can view conversations i.e. groups of emails on the same subject. There is also a facility for showing your own replies within a conversation. To view a conversation:

1. Select View>Organize by Conversation from the Mail menu bar

2. Emails with the same subject are grouped together as a conversation in the left-hand pane. The number of grouped emails is shown at the right-hand side

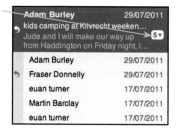

3. Click here to view the full list of emails

4. The full conversation is shown in the right-hand pane

5. Click on this button to include your own messages in a conversation

6. Click on this button to hide your own messages in a conversation

# Attaching Photos

Emails do not have to be restricted to plain text. Through the use of attachments they can also include other documents and particularly photos. This is an excellent way to send photos to family and friends around the world. There are two ways to attach photos to an email:

### Attach button
To attach photos using the Attach button:

1 Click on this icon on the Mail toolbar

**146**

2 Browse your hard drive for the photo(s) you want to include in your email. Select the photos you want

3 Click on the Choose File button

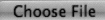

4 The photo is added to the body of the email

## Photo Browser

To attach photos using the Photo Browser:

**1** Click on this icon on the Mail toolbar

**2** Browse the Photo Browser for the photo(s) that you want to include

**Don't forget**

The Photo Browser is available from a variety of other applications.

**3** Drag the selected photo(s) into the open email to include them in the message

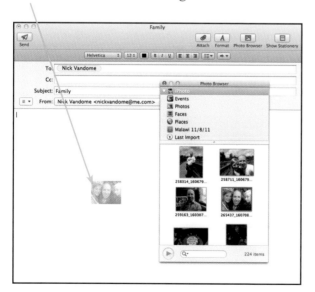

# Email Stationery

You do not have to settle for conservative formatting options in emails and Mail offers a variety of templates that can give your messages a creative and eye-catching appearance. It can also be used to format any photos that you have attached to your message. This is done through the use of the Stationery function. To use this:

**1** Click on this icon on the Mail toolbar

**2** Select a category for the stationery

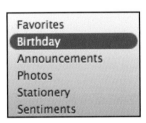

**3** Double-click on a style to apply it to the email

**4** The stationery incorporates any photos that have been attached from the Photo Browser

# Dealing with Junk Email

Spam, or junk email, is the scourge of every email user. It is unwanted and unsolicited messages that are usually sent in bulk to lists of email addresses. In Mail there is a function to try and limit the amount of junk email that you receive in your Inbox. To do this:

**1** When you receive a junk email, click on this button on the Mail toolbar (initially this will help to train Mail to identify junk email)

**2** Once Mail has recognized the types of junk that you receive it will start to filter them directly into the Junk Mailbox

**Hot tip**

It is worth occasionally checking in your Junk Mailbox, in case something you want has been put there.

149

**3** To set the preferences for junk email select Mail>Preferences from the Menu bar and click on the Junk tab

**4** Junk email is displayed in the Junk Mailbox

# Text and Video Chatting

One issue with email is that you can never be sure when the recipient receives the message, or when they will reply to it. For a more immediate form of communication, instant message or video messaging can be used. This is done with the iChat program. To use this:

**1** Click on this icon on the Dock

**2** In order to chat to someone you have to add them as a buddy. To do this, click on this button

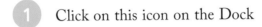

**3** Select the required contact from your Address Book

**4** Select a buddy in the iChat window

**5** Click on this button to start a text chat

**6** Click on this button to start a video chat

# 9 Mac Mobility

*This chapter shows how
Apple has revolutionized
the way we use mobile
computing devices.*

# iPhone

Launched in 2007, the iPhone is one of the products that has helped propel Apple to be the world's most valuable technology company. It is a smartphone that is capable of accessing the Web, using email, taking photos, recording videos and playing multimedia content such as music and movies. In essence it is really a mini computer that can also be used to make phone calls and send and receive texts.

The user interface of the iPhone is a touchscreen with a virtual keypad, rather than the traditional screen and physical keypad. The screen is navigated around by using swiping gestures with your fingers and tapping to access items. These multi-touch gestures have now been incorporated into OS X Lion for desktop Macs and MacBooks.

**Don't forget**

The iPhone partly made its name by the huge range of apps that quickly became available after its launch. These can be downloaded from the Mac App Store and cover pretty much everything you ever wanted to do on a smartphone.

At the time of writing, the current iPhone is the 4S. Some of its features are:

- Dual-core A5 processor chip

- 8 mega pixel camera

- 1080p HD video recording

- Siri, intelligent voice assistant

- iOS 5. This is the operating system for Apple's mobile devices including the iPhone, iPad and iPod Touch

- iCloud. This is an online service that enables you to store your content in the iCloud (see pages 155–158 for more details)

# iPad

Apple have a knack of changing the way people look at computers and computing and the iPad was another product that continued this trend. It is a tablet computer that is primarily designed for multimedia content, such as movies, video games, music and books, but it can also be used for productivity options such as word processing or creating presentations and spreadsheets.

The first iPad was released in 2010 and operates in a similar way to the iPhone, with a large touchscreen and a virtual keyboard that appears when you need to type anything. All iPads come with Wi-Fi connectivity for access to the Web and some models have 3G connectivity so that you can connect to the Internet in the same way as you would with an iPhone.

The majority of programs for the iPad can be downloaded from the Mac App Store, in the same way as for the iPhone and Mac computers.

The current version of the iPad is iPad 2 and some of its features are:

- Dual-core A5 processor chip

- Two cameras, one on the front and one on the back

- Up to 10 hour battery life

- Instant On. Turns on from sleep immediately

- iOS 5

- iCloud

**Don't forget**

iPad 2 comes with a Smart Cover. This is a firm cover that protects the iPad and it can also be used to support it by folding it behind the iPad. The Smart Covers come in a range of colors.

# iOS 5

iOS 5 is the latest operating system for the mobile Apple devices: iPhone, iPad and iPod Touch. Because they are required to operate differently from computers, mobile devices need a different type of operating system. However, with iOS 5 it is possible to ensure that your mobile devices can also be used in conjunction with any of your Mac computers. iOS 5 is a robust operating system that has a wealth of features for all of your mobile computing needs.

## Features

Some of the features of iOS 5 are

- Enhanced Safari Web browser

- Improved photo editing

- iMessage. Free messaging with other Mac users

- Notification Center for all of your online alerts

- Improved syncing with your email and calendar

- Game Center for one of the best mobile gaming experiences

- New multi-touch gestures for accessing content

- Direct integration with Twitter

- Newsstand, for any online newspaper or magazine subscriptions that you may have

- Integration with iCloud (see next page)

# iCloud

Cloud computing is an attractive proposition and one that has gained greatly in popularity in recent years. As a concept, it consists of storing your content on an external computer server. This not only gives you added security in terms of backing up your information, it also means that the content can then be shared over a variety of mobile devices.

iCloud is Apple's consumer cloud computing product and one that will replace the MobileMe service. This consists of online services such as email, a calendar, contacts and a documents. iCloud was introduced in the fall/autumn 2011 and MobileMe will be phased out by June 2012. MobileMe users will be able to migrate to the new iCloud service, which will be free for the standard package.

iCloud provides users with a way to save their files and apps to the online service and then use them across their mobile devices such as iPhones, iPads and iPod Touches.

## About iCloud

iCloud can be accessed from this icon:

You can use iCloud to save and share the following:

- Music

- Photos

- Documents

- Apps

- Books

- Backups

- Contacts and calendars

When you save an item to the iCloud it automatically pushes it to all of your other compatible devices; you do not have to manually sync anything, iCloud does it all for you.

# Using iCloud

To use iCloud you have to first ensure that all of your devices meet the required specifications.

### Setting up a computer

To use iCloud on a Mac desktop or a MacBook, OS X Lion 10.7.2, or higher, is required. To upgrade from OS X Lion 10.7 to 10.7.2:

**Don't forget**

To use iTunes and iPhoto with iCloud, you need to have iTunes 10.5, or later, and iPhone 9.2, or later, in order to share your music and photos.

**1** Click on the Apple menu and click on Software Update…

**2** Select the required software update (Mac OS X Update Combined) and click on the Install button. The update will be installed automatically but you will be prompted to restart your Mac during the process

**Don't forget**

Music and photos are not included in your 5GB storage limit on iCloud. This only includes emails, documents, account information, Camera Roll (for saved or edited photos) and account settings.

**3** Once OS X Lion has been upgraded to 10.7.2, open the System Preferences and click on the iCloud button under the Internet & Wireless section

iCloud

**4** To use iCloud you will need an Apple ID. Enter the details for this and click on the Sign In button

**5** If you have an existing MobileMe account you will be prompted to update it to iCloud. Click on the Move... button to be taken through a wizard for moving to iCloud

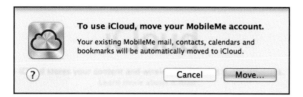

**Don't forget**

Once you have set up iCloud, you can login to the online service at www.icloud.com/ This consists of your online email service, your contacts and your calendar. You can login to your iCloud account from any Internet-enabled device.

**6** Once you have joined iCloud, click on the iCloud button in System Preferences

**7** Check on the services that you want to use with iCloud. These will then be updated automatically on all of your iCloud enabled devices

**Hot tip**

Whenever you take a photo with an iPhone, iPad or iPod Touch, it will be sent to all other devices via Photo Stream. This also happens when you import new photos into iPhoto (providing you have an Internet connection). To use existing photos in iPhoto, just drag them from the main window onto the Photo Stream button. A master copy of all your photos is kept on your Mac desktop or MacBook.

**8** To manage your photos with iCloud, open iPhoto and click on the Photo Stream button

**9** Click on the Turn On Photo Stream to activate it to manage your photos over all of your devices

...cont'd

## Setting up devices
To use iCloud with iPhones, iPads and iPod Touches:

**1** Ensure your device is operating with iOS 5

**2** Sign in with your Apple ID or create a new one

**3** Turn on iCloud by dragging this button to the On position

**4** Select the settings for your device and turn on the options you want to use with iCloud

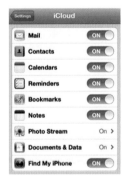

## How iCloud works
Once you have installed iCloud on all of your devices it will automatically update all of your selected content without you having to do anything. So, for instance, if you buy music from iTunes on your iPad, it will automatically also be available on your iPhone and MacBook. Similarly, if you buy a new app from the Mac App Store, or update your calendar or address book details, this will be updated across all of your iCloud-enabled devices.

# 10 Expanding Your Horizons

*This chapter shows how you can develop your skills on a Mac, from adding new users to setting up a network of computers.*

# Adding Users

Due to the power and versatility of Macs it would seem a shame to limit their use to a single person. Thankfully, it is possible to set up user accounts for several people on the same Mac. This means that each person can log in to their own settings and preferences. All user accounts can be password protected, to ensure that each user's environment is secure. To set up multiple user accounts:

**1** Click on the System Preferences icon on the Dock

**2** Click on the Users & Groups icon

**Don't forget**

Each user can select their own icon or photo of themselves.

**3** The information about the current account is displayed. This is your own account and the information is based on details you provided when you first set up your Mac

**4** Click on this icon to enable new accounts to be added (the padlock needs to be open)

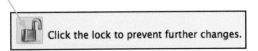

**5** Click on the plus sign icon to add a new account

**6** Enter the details for the new account holder

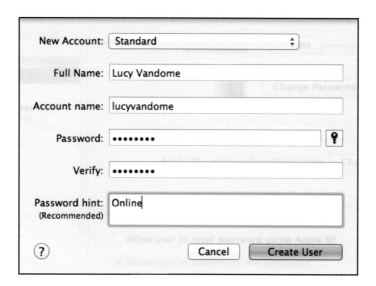

**Don't forget**

By default, you are the administrator of your own Mac. This means that you can create, edit and delete other user accounts.

161

**7** Click on the Create User button

**8** The new account is added to the list in the Accounts window, under Other Users

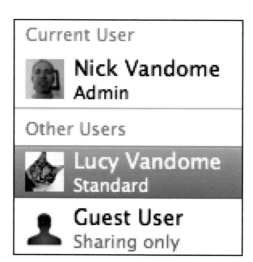

# Login Options

Once you have set up more than one user you can determine what happens at login i.e. when the Mac is turned on. You may want to display a list of all of the users for that machine, or you may want to have yourself logged in automatically. To set login options:

1 Click on the System Preferences icon on the Dock

2 Click on the Users & Groups icon

Users & Groups

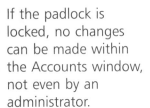
3 Click on the padlock to open it

4 Click on the Login Options button

Login Options

5 The Login Options window allows you to select settings for when you turn on your Mac

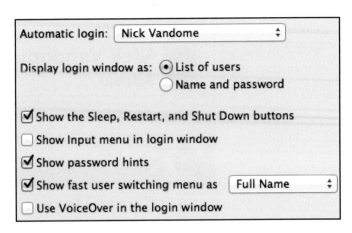

Automatic login: Nick Vandome

Display login window as: ● List of users
○ Name and password

☑ Show the Sleep, Restart, and Shut Down buttons
☐ Show Input menu in login window
☑ Show password hints
☑ Show fast user switching menu as  Full Name
☐ Use VoiceOver in the login window

**6** Click on the Automatic login box

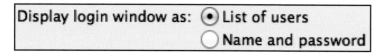

**Hot tip**

If Automatic Login is selected for a named user, no username or password needs to be selected when the Mac is turned on.

**7** Select a name from the list. (If Off is selected all of the users for that Mac will be displayed at login)

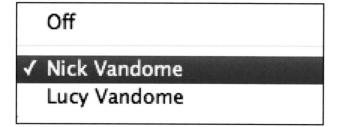

**8** If Off is selected, select one of the options for how the login window is displayed

Display login window as: ● List of users
○ Name and password

**9** Check on this box if you want to make it as easy as possible to switch between users (see next page)

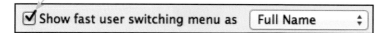

☑ Show fast user switching menu as   Full Name ⇕

# Switching Between Users

If there are multiple users set up on a Mac it is useful to be able to switch between them as quickly as possible.
When this is done, the first user's session is retained so that they can return to it if required. To switch between users:

**1** Make sure Fast User Switching is enabled (see previous page)

☑ **Show fast user switching menu as** | Full Name ⬍ |

**2** At the top-right of the screen, click on the current user's name

**Nick Vandome**

**3** Click on the name of another user

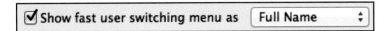
rged) Sun 17:05 | Nick Vandome
Lucy Vandome
✓ Nick Vandome

**164**

**4** Enter the relevant password (if required)

Lucy Vandome

••••••••

**5** Click on the arrow to login

# Parental Controls

Children, and grandchildren, love computers and it is not always possible to fully monitor what they are doing on them. Therefore, it is useful to be able to put in some system controls if you have any user accounts for younger members of the family. To do this:

1. Click on the System Preferences icon on the Dock

2. Click on the Parental Controls icon

3. Select a user account to which you want to apply controls. By default, Parental Controls are turned off

4. Check on this button to enable Parental Controls in the Users & Groups System Preferences

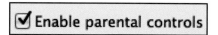

...cont'd

## Apps controls

**1** Click on the Apps tab

**2** Check on the Use Simple Finder box to show a simplified version of the Finder

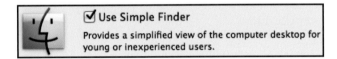
☑ Use Simple Finder
Provides a simplified view of the computer desktop for young or inexperienced users.

**3** Check on this box if you want to limit the types of program that a user can access

166

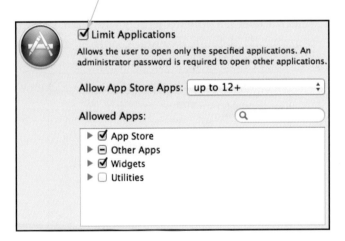

**4** Check off the boxes next to the programs that you do not want used

**5** Click here to select options for age limits in terms of access items in the App Store

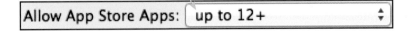
Allow App Store Apps: up to 12+

## Web controls

**1**    Click on the Web tab

**2**    Check on this button to try to prevent access to websites with adult content

**3**    Check on this button to specify specific websites that are suitable to be viewed

## People controls

**1**    Click on the People tab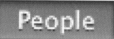

**2**    Check on the Limit boxes to limit the type of content in email messages and iChat text messages

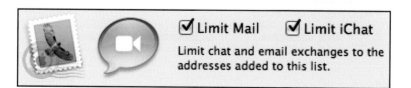

**Don't forget**

iChat is a Mac program for instant text and video messaging.

...cont'd

**3** The Allowed Contacts box enables you to enter details of people who you want to be able to contact the user via email or iChat

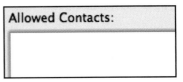

**4** Click on this button to add new contacts

**5** Enter details of the contacts or click on this button to access Address Book contact

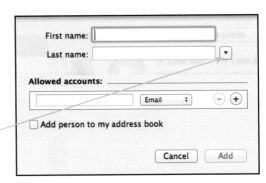

**6** Select a contact and click on the Add button

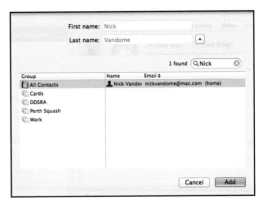

**7** The selected contact is displayed in the Allowed Contacts window

## Time controls

**1** Click on the Time Limits tab **Time Limits**

**2** Check on this box to limit the amount of time the user can use the Mac during weekdays

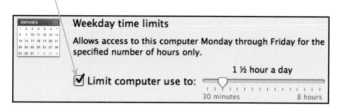

**3** Check on this box to limit the amount of time the user can use the Mac during weekends

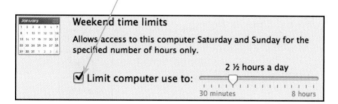

**4** Check on these boxes to determine the times at which the user cannot access their account

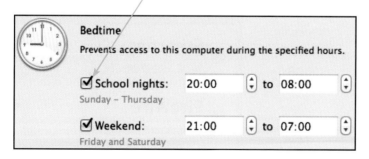

# Creating Your Own Network

Computer networks are two or more computers joined together to share information. A computer connected to the Internet constitutes a network, as does one computer connected to another.

Networks can be set up by joining computers together with cables or wirelessly. The latter is becoming more and more common and this can be done with a wireless router and a wireless card in the computer. New Macs come with wireless cards installed so it is just a case of buying a wireless router. (Apple sell their own version of this, known as Airport.) A wireless router connects to your telephone line and then you can set up your Mac, or Macs, to join the network and communicate with each other and the Internet. To do this:

**Don't forget**

Wireless routers should automatically detect a wireless card in a Mac.

1   Click on the System Preferences icon on the Dock

2   Click on the Network icon

3   The Network window displays the current settings

4   Click on the Assist Me button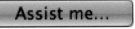

**5** The Network Setup Assistant is launched

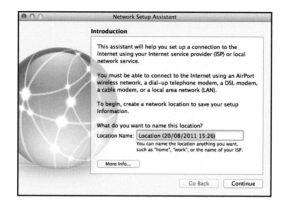

**6** Enter a name for your network connection

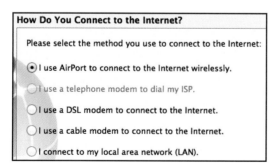

**7** Click on the Continue button  **Continue**

**8** Select how you connect to the Internet

**How Do You Connect to the Internet?**

Please select the method you use to connect to the Internet:

- ⦿ I use AirPort to connect to the Internet wirelessly.
- ◯ I use a telephone modem to dial my ISP.
- ◯ I use a DSL modem to connect to the Internet.
- ◯ I use a cable modem to connect to the Internet.
- ◯ I connect to my local area network (LAN).

**9** Click on the Continue button  **Continue**

...cont'd

**10** Select the name of your wireless router

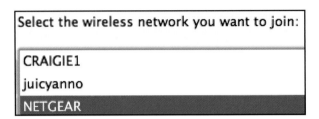

Select the wireless network you want to join:

CRAIGIE1

juicyanno

NETGEAR

**11** Enter the password for the router. This will have been set when you installed the router

Password: Selected network requires a password

••••••••

**12** Click on the Continue button

Continue

**13** The Ready to Connect window confirms that you are ready to connect to your router

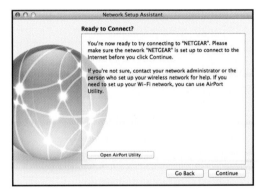

**14** Click on the Continue button

Continue

# Sharing on a Network

One of the main reasons for creating a network of two or more computers is to share files between them.
On networked Macs, this involves setting them up so that they can share files and then accessing these files.

## Setting up file sharing

To set up file sharing on a networked Mac:

**1** Click on the System Preference icon on the Dock

**2** Click on the Sharing icon

Sharing

**3** Check on the boxes next to the items you want to share (the most common items to share are files and printers)

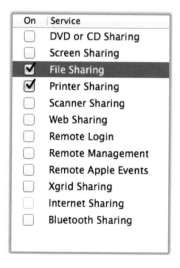

| On | Service |
|----|---------|
| ☐ | DVD or CD Sharing |
| ☐ | Screen Sharing |
| ☑ | File Sharing |
| ☑ | Printer Sharing |
| ☐ | Scanner Sharing |
| ☐ | Web Sharing |
| ☐ | Remote Login |
| ☐ | Remote Management |
| ☐ | Remote Apple Events |
| ☐ | Xgrid Sharing |
| ☐ | Internet Sharing |
| ☐ | Bluetooth Sharing |

### Don't forget

If you only use your network to connect to the Internet then you do not need to worry about file sharing. This is mainly for sharing files between two different computers.

**4** Click on the padlock to close it and prevent more changes

## ...cont'd

### Accessing other computers

When you access other computers on a network you do so as either a registered user or a guest. If you are a registered user it usually means you are accessing another computer of which you are an administrator i.e. the main user. This gives you greater access to the computer's contents than if you are a guest. To access another computer on your network:

1 Networked computers should show up automatically in the Finder. Double-click on one to access it

2 By default, you will be connected as a Guest, with limited access. Click on the Connect As... button in the Finder window

3 Click on Registered User button

4 Enter your name and the password for the computer to which you want to connect (this will be your user password on that computer)

**Don't forget**

When connecting to another computer, it has to be turned on.

5 Click on the Connect button

**Connect**

6 In the Finder you will have access to the hard drive of the networked computer

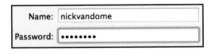

7 You will then be able to access files and folders in the same way as if they were on the computer on which you are viewing them

## Guest users

Guest users on a network are users other than yourself, or other registered users, to whom you want to limit access to your files and folders. Guests only have access to a folder called the Drop Box in your own Public folder. To share files with Guest users you have to first copy them into the Drop Box. To do this:

**1** Create a file and select File>Save from the Menu bar

**2** Navigate to your own home folder (this is created automatically by OS X and displayed in the Finder Sidebar)

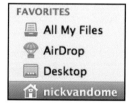

**Don't forget**

Your home folder is the one with your Mac username.

**3** Double-click on the Public folder

**4** Double-click on the Drop Box folder

**5** Save the file into the Drop Box

...cont'd

### Accessing a Drop Box

To access files in a Drop Box:

**1** Double-click on a networked computer in the Finder

**2** Click on the Connect As button in the Finder window

**3** Click on the Guest button

**4** Click on the Connect button

**Connect**

**5** Double-click on the administrator's folder

**6** Double-click on the Drop Box folder to access the files within it

# 11  Safety Net

This chapter shows some of the ways in which you can keep your Mac, and your files, safe and secure.

# Mac Security

Modern computers are plagued by viruses, spyware and malware, all of which can corrupt data or impair the smooth running of the system. Thankfully, Macs are less prone to this than computers running Windows, partly due to the fact that there are a smaller number of Macs for the virus writers to worry about and partly because the UNIX system on which the Mac OS X is based is a very robust platform.

However, this is not to say that Mac users should be complacent in the face of potential attacks. In order to try and minimize the threat of viruses and unwanted visitors try some of the following steps:

- Install anti-virus software and a firewall. Although this is not as essential as for a computer running Windows it will give you additional peace of mind. Norton and Sophos produce good anti-virus software for the Mac

- Protect your Mac with a password. This means that no-one can log on without the required password

- Download software updates from Apple, which, among other things, contain security updates (see next page)

- Do not open suspicious email attachments

- In Safari, select Safari>Preferences and click on the Security tab. Deselect any items that you feel may put your computer at risk

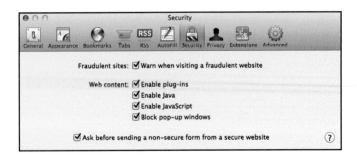

# Updating Software

Apple periodically releases updates for its software: both its programs and the OS X operating system. The latter are probably more important as they contain security fixes for the system that have come to light. To update software:

1. Click on the System Preferences icon on the Dock

2. Click on the Software Update icon

3. Click on the Check Now button to view available updates

4. Check on the boxes next to the updates you want to install

### Don't forget

If checks are set automatically, you will be alerted, at the specified time, whenever updates are available and you can choose whether to install them or not.

5. Click on the Install button

6. Check on the Check for Updates box to have updates checked for automatically

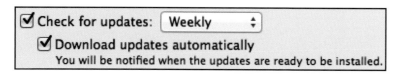

# Checking Your System

Macs have a couple of programs that can be used to check the overall health and condition of your system. These are utilities called Activity Monitor and System Information. To access these programs:

**1** In the Finder click on the Applications button or access it from the Launchpad

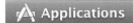

**2** Double-click on the Utilities folder

**3** Double-click on either program to open it

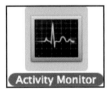

## Activity Monitor

This can be used to check how much memory is being used up on your Mac, and also by certain programs:

**1** Click on the CPU tab to see how much processor memory is being used up

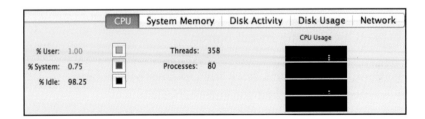

2. Click on the System Memory tab to see how much system memory (RAM) is being used up

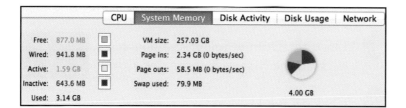

**Don't forget**

RAM is the memory that is used to open and run programs. The more RAM you have the more efficiently your Mac will run.

3. Click on the Disk Usage tab to see how much space has been taken up on the hard drive

4. Double-click on a program to see its individual details

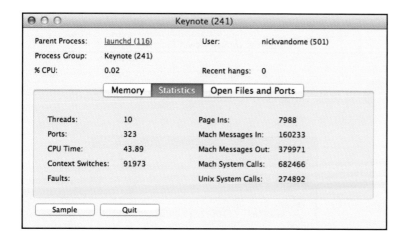

...cont'd

## System Information

This can be used to view how the different hardware and software elements on your Mac are performing. To do this:

**1** Open the Utilities folder and double-click on the System Information icon

**2** Click on the Hardware link and click on an item of hardware

> ▼ Hardware
>   ATA
>   Audio (Built In)
>   Bluetooth
>   Card Reader
>   Diagnostics
>   Disc Burning

**3** Details about the item of hardware, and its performance, are displayed

| MATSHITA DVD-R UJ-898: | |
|---|---|
| Firmware Revision: | HE13 |
| Interconnect: | ATAPI |
| Burn Support: | Yes (Apple Shipping Drive) |
| Cache: | 1024 KB |
| Reads DVD: | Yes |
| CD-Write: | -R, -RW |
| DVD-Write: | -R, -R DL, -RW, +R, +R DL, +RW |
| Write Strategies: | CD-TAO, CD-SAO, DVD-DAO |
| Media: | To show the available burn speeds, insert a disc and choose View > Refresh |

**4** Click on software items to view their details

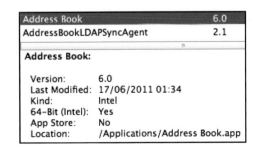

# Dealing with Crashes

Although Macs are rightly known for their stability, there are occasions when something goes wrong and a program crashes or freezes. This is usually denoted by a spinning colored ball (known as the Spinning Beach Ball of Death). Only rarely will you have to turn off your Mac and turn it on again to resolve the problem. Usually, Force Quit can be used to close down the affected program. To do this:

1. Once the spinning ball appears, click on the Apple Menu

2. Select Force Quit from the Apple Menu

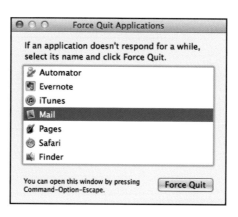

or

1. Hold down the Command (Apple), Alt and Esc keys at the same time

2. Click on the non-responding program

3. Click on the Force Quit button

**Don't forget**

It is unusual for Macs to freeze completely. However, if this does happen, hold down the start button for a few seconds until your Mac turns off. You should then be able to start it normally.

**183**

# Backing Up

Backing up data on your Mac is a chore, but it is an essential one: if the worst comes to the worst and all of your data is corrupted or lost then you will be very grateful that you went to the trouble of backing it up. Macs have a number of options for backing up data.

### Burning discs

One of the most traditional methods of backing up data is to burn it onto a disc that can then be stored elsewhere. These days this is most frequently done on CDs or DVDs. To do this:

**Don't forget**

The CD/DVD burner on a Mac is known as a SuperDrive.

**184**

① Insert the CD/DVD into the CD/DVD slot

② Select for the disc to be shown in the Finder

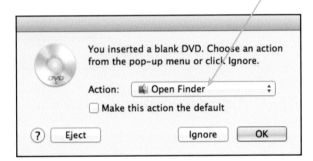

You inserted a blank DVD. Choose an action from the pop-up menu or click Ignore.

Action:    Open Finder

☐ Make this action the default

(?)   [ Eject ]      [ Ignore ]   [ OK ]

**Hot tip**

If a CD or DVD does not burn successfully, try a different brand of discs. Sometimes the coating on some discs can cause a problem with the disc burner.

③ Locate the item you want to copy

Pictures

④ Drag it onto the disc name in the Finder

⑤ Click on this icon to burn the disc

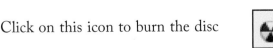

## Time Machine

Time Machine is a feature of OS X that gives you great peace of mind. In conjunction with an external hard drive, it creates a backup of your whole system, including folders, files, programs and even the OS X operating system itself.

Once it has been set up, Time Machine takes a backup every hour and you can then go into Time Machine to restore any files that have been deleted or become corrupt.

## Setting up Time Machine

To use Time Machine it has to first be set up. This involves attaching a hard drive to your Mac. To set up Time Machine:

**Beware**

If an external hard drive is not attached to your Mac you will not be able to use Time Machine and a warning message will appear when you try to set it up.

185

**1** Click on the Time Machine icon on the Dock or access it in the System Preferences

**2** You will be prompted to set up Time Machine

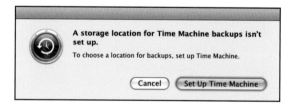

**3** Click on the Set Up Time Machine button

**4** In the Time Machine System Preferences window, click on the Choose Backup Disk... button

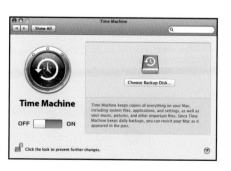

## ...cont'd

**5** Connect an external hard drive and select it

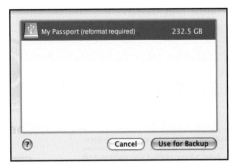

**6** Click on the Use for Backup button

**7** In the Time Machine System Preferences window, drag the button to the On position

**8** The backup will begin. The initial backup copies your whole system and can take several hours. Subsequent hourly backups only look at items that have been changed since the previous backup

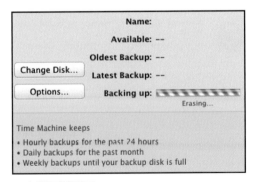

**9** The progress of the backup is displayed in the System Preferences window and also here

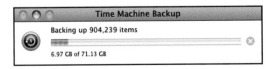

# Index